Developing Faithful Ministers

Developing Faithful Ministers

A Practical and Theological Handbook

Edited by

Tim Ling and Lesley Bentley

scm press

© The editors and contributors

Published in 2012 by SCM Press
Editorial office
3rd Floor, Invicta House, Golden Lane
London, EC1Y OTG, UK

SCM Press is an imprint of Hymns Ancient & Modern Ltd (a registered charity)
13A Hellesdon Park Road
Norwich NR6 5DR, UK
www.scmpress.co.uk

The Authors have asserted their right under the Copyright, Designs and Patents
Act, 1988,
to be identified as the Authors of this Work

British Library Cataloguing in Publication data

A catalogue record for this book is available
from the British Library

978-0-334-04383-6
Kindle edition 978-0-334-04468-0

Typeset by The Manila Typesetting Company
Printed and bound by
CPI Group, Croydon

Contents

Contributors

Simon Baker is Director of Discipleship and Ministry in the Winchester Diocese.

Paul Bayes is the Bishop of Hertford and formerly the Church of England's National Adviser for Mission and Evangelism.

Lesley Bentley is the Director of Ministry in the Lichfield Diocese and a member of the Church of England's National Advisory Panel that supports the Continuing Ministerial Development of licensed ministers. Formerly Team Rector of Bilton in the Diocese of Ripon and Leeds, she is the book's co-editor.

Stuart Burns is Head of the School for Ministry in the Leicester Diocese and co-author of *Saints on Earth* (Church House Publishing, 2004).

Stephen Cherry is the Director of Ministerial Development and Parish Support in the Durham Diocese and author of *Barefoot Disciple: Walking the Way of Passionate Humility* (Continuum, 2011).

Sue Cross is the former Head of Adult Learning and Professional Development at University College London and author of *Adult Teaching and Learning – Developing Your Practice* (McGraw Hill, 2009).

Neville Emslie is the Ministry Development Officer in the Canterbury Diocese. He is author of *The Minister as Poet* (School of Ministry, Knox College, 2002).

Neil Evans is Director of Ministry for the London Diocese.

Tim Ling is the Church of England's National Adviser for Continuing Ministerial Development and the book's co-editor.

CONTRIBUTORS

Roger Matthews is Director of Mission and Ministry in the Chelmsford Diocese, a member of the Church of England's National Advisory Panel that supports the Continuing Ministerial Development of licensed ministers, and a trustee of The Leadership Institute.

Andrew Mayes is Diocesan Spirituality Adviser in the Chichester Diocese and author of *Spirituality in Ministerial Formation: The Dynamic of Prayer in Learning* (University of Wales Press, 2010).

David Parrott is educational adviser to the Ecclesiastical Law Society and author of *Your Church and the Law* (Canterbury Press, 2nd edn. 2011).

John Preston is National Stewardship and Resources Officer for the Church of England and author of *The Money Revolution: Applying Christian Principles to Handling Your Money* (Authentic Media, 2007).

Introduction

This book aims to support the work of all those involved in supervision and training relationships within the Church. Its primary relevance will be for training ministers and curates or licensed lay ministers in training. The book's title *Developing Faithful Ministers* draws attention to our view that this is not an instrumental activity but rather one that is rooted in God's faithfulness. The Church is called upon to proclaim afresh in each generation the good news of this faithfulness. This present generation of ministers, as with each new generation, has to face particular challenges. The primary challenge is to grow in that which we profess, God's love, to learn to love the world in the pattern of Christ, and to live through the renewing power of the Holy Spirit. Alternatively put, we might say that the challenge for this generation is to get serious about God's mission in late-Christendom. The secondary challenges are more mundane. The Church of England has historically regarded itself as having a responsibility for the whole nation. Changing public attitudes mean that the Church is now frequently seen as part of the 'Third Sector' providing a service to client groups, and there is an assumption of professionalism in service and behaviour. In parallel, particularly within a Church of England context, in response to section 23 of the Employment Relations Act, there is now an expectation of demonstrable capability prior to being licensed to any form of permanent tenure. The demand for more professional, demonstrably capable, mission able and collaborative licensed ministers places particular weight on the efficacy of the initial training relationship. This book seeks to support those who find themselves in these relationships by offering both theological reflection on what these challenges might mean for developing ministry and models of good practice.

Form and content

The book takes the form of a collection of essays each written by a different author who brings particular experience and expertise to the subject at hand. These have been arranged thematically into three sections.

The first section broadly addresses the theme of faithfulness, with three chapters that reflect on the nature of confidence, community and creativity as they relate to ministry and its development. Neville Emslie starts by encouraging us to explore what it means to have confidence in a God who calls us from comfort to discomfort, to discover that Jesus himself is already there, and to realize that in him and towards him lies our confidence. Paul Bayes continues the theme by helping us to consider how we may live out our espoused ecclesiology, as a loving community of friends, in a world that demands professional clarity. Andrew Mayes concludes the section by answering his own question 'What is formation?' by pointing to God's creativity in us. We are formed by Word, worship, woundedness and wonder.

The second section focuses on the developmental context with three chapters that provide both theoretical and practical resources to support the learning relationship between the training minister and the curate. First, Sue Cross explores the various dimensions that make up the teacher–learner relationship. She argues that better teaching ultimately comes from the degree to which the teacher is open to finding the relationship a source of 'deeper satisfaction, greater challenge, and by no means least, more fun'. Second, Roger Matthews leads us on a tour through history, disciplines and traditions, to reflect on the power of asking questions. He then moves from reflection to practice by outlining five methods of personal and organizational development built around the use of questions. The section concludes with Stuart Burns' chapter that helps us to get behind the rhetoric of 'reflective practice' by exploring what sorts of conversations may really be taking place to support learning. He offers two tools to evaluate this practice and to align future conversations to enable a more creative critical engagement.

The final section addresses more directly approaches to, and practicalities in, the exercise of ministry. Stephen Cherry starts this section by reflecting on how we make use of time in the context of the 'various and fluctuating demands of ministry'. His chapter offers a model that supplements 'time management' with 'time wisdom'. Lesley Bentley continues by appealing for us to imagine ministry beyond a succession of pastoral tasks and to explore it through the lens of enabling others. With practical suggestions from parish settings she advocates an approach to ministry that is about modelling discipleship, enabling ministry, and holding the vision. Simon Baker moves us on by encouraging us in our approach to the preaching ministry to seek to discover our authentic voice, and in our exploration to be attentive not only to the Spirit in prayer, but also to the word of God in Scripture and the life of the community. He provides case studies and exercises to support our journey of discovery.

The remaining chapters of this section focus on the practicalities of money, law and meetings. John Preston challenges the sacred and secular divide that sometimes characterizes approaches to money. He argues that clergy should take a lead in matters of finance as it is essentially a spiritual subject. Indeed, he demonstrates this, while providing practical advice, by illustrating how it touches on questions of personal lifestyles, church administration and resourcing of mission, as well as the offering of ourselves in worship. David Parrott continues the unapologetic tone in advocating the importance of attending to the practicalities in ministry. In his chapter he sets out concisely and in plain English the whys and wherefores of church law – and its significance for mission. Neil Evans concludes by sharing his belief that meetings can be constructive, interesting, entertaining and fruitful occasions and that it is possible to set up meetings to help enable these outcomes. His chapter offers a series of practical suggestions to help make this possibility a reality.

The book concludes with an essay on Continuing Professional Development by Tim Ling that reflects, in light of the preceding chapters, on the nature and condition of ministry today. It argues that in our wrestling with professional and ministerial identities we are neither innovators nor lost but rather that through God's grace we find ourselves in a long line of men and women, faithful pilgrims, seeking to grow in his love.

How you might read this book

Some books are to be tasted, others to be swallowed, and some few to be chewed and digested; that is, some books are to be read only in parts; others to be read, but not curiously; and some few to be read wholly, and with diligence and attention. (Sir Francis Bacon (1561–1626), *Of Studies*[1])

This is a multi-author volume and by analogy to Francis Bacon we do not imagine that all chapters in this volume will receive the same sorts of attention. Indeed we suspect that depending on your context how you might read the book will change over time. However, we primarily imagine three sorts of readings:

1. Reading in order to engage in theological reflection on the training you are supporting or are engaged in, for example attempting to make sense of the apparently espoused theology of ministry that has

---

1 http://www.authorama.com/essays-of-francis-bacon-50.html (accessed 6th January 2012).

characterized your training so far and that which you are experiencing in practice.

2. Reading in the hope of finding some immediate help in addressing a particular issue in a training relationship, for example how to move from being nice to becoming real in your conversations with your new curate or incumbent.

3. Reading with a view to learning more about practical issues in ministry, for example how to chair meetings better following the less than discreet feedback that you've just received from the parish treasurer.

Broadly speaking the sections of the book and the chapter headings will point you in the right direction and provide ample material for you to bring into dialogue with your own experiences. However, we encourage you not to view these headings too prescriptively. We would not wish to make any crude distinction between the practical and the theological. Finally, we have already made reference to the 'more mundane', and imagine one last reader who may be looking to find evidence that they're 'demonstrably capable'. This is a practical and honourable task. It is also one that this book will help you with. Lesley Bentley has produced an Appendix, *Learning Outcomes Exercises*, setting out on how chapters of the book might help you to explore the House of Bishops' Learning Outcomes (2005) which have become an important part of Initial Ministerial Education 4–7 and the assessment of the end of curacy.

PART I

Faithfulness

Confidence in Calling

NEVILLE EMSLIE

Culture and context

While there are still a few golf and social clubs in the land that are 'male-only', there is a club in the UK that is far more difficult to gain admission to. Business people, sportsmen and women, artists, politicians and ministers strive mightily to enter this most restricted of British clubs, *Club Confidence*. Ironically *Club Confidence* has many members but almost all who seek to enter would agree that its present incumbents are illegitimate gatecrashers, people who have barged in via the backdoor of celebrity or squalid self-aggrandizement or self-endorsement. Mark Twain once said that 'all you need in this life is ignorance and confidence, and then success is sure'.

For some years I have played a game with my wife as we read the newspaper or watch the news on television. How far does one read, or how long will it be, until the word 'confidence' is used? Invariably it occurs by page two in the front section of the newspaper, and it is certainly on the first page of the business and sports sections.[1] I typed the word 'confidence' in the search box of a major online Sunday newspaper and received 54,570 results. On the TV news the word generally occurs in the first five minutes.

Generally the word is prefaced by 'crisis in', or 'if we had more'. I notice that when the PM says of a cabinet colleague, 'I have every confidence in the Minister', it means if the Minister does not resign today, he or she will be sacked tomorrow. The gatecrashers of *Club Confidence* described above appear to have immense confidence in their beautiful visage, or their ability to kick a round ball accurately, or to play three chords on an electric guitar extremely enthusiastically. Their confidence lies *in* something, a feature or an ability.

---

1 For instance the opening sentence of a recent lead editorial titled 'Summer of Discontent' is, 'The peculiar confidence of the British is a thing often understated, but rarely absent', *The Times*, Thursday 11th August 2011, p. 2.

What can be said about the Christian minister? *Club Confidence* does not have many paid-up ordained members, or those that are seem to be rampant extraverts, brash leaders or just plain dangerous. On the other hand we admire the Christian leader that stands against the majority view, or commands respect through force of personality, rigorous logic or exegetical insight. There can be theological clashes of course, as disciples of Jesus are meant to be people of humility, and the 'do unto others' ethic subverts the type of confidence that pushes to the front of the queue.

Ministry and confidence

The minister's work is particularly complex for the minister works in multimedia, all the while endeavouring to bring fellow human beings to attend to that which is ineffable, mysterious and transcendent, yet ground in the dirt and dust of this short existence. I have argued elsewhere that ministers are poets, and that ordination sets apart these ones for the artistry of constructing word and thought, liturgy and imagination, time and space, symbol and metaphor, silence and sound to facilitate encounter with God.[2] Ministers join with artists – sculptors, painters, installation artists, novelists, poets – seeking to describe what it means to be human.

In the first place the minister must learn to attend. She must listen with highly attuned ear to the voices on the wind, and must look intently for all colours in the soul. With the poet the minister needs a confidence in life that moves into the future. This is the prophetic task, to which all artists and ministers are called: to see and believe in what is to come, and to call others to attend to this together. John Zizioulas speaks of 'the word' coming 'not from the past but from the future; it is an echo of things to come',[3] and the same foresight was a striking feature of the poet William Stafford; the ability to see ahead which better enables present apprehension, as in his poem 'Yes'[4]

It could happen any time, tornado,
earthquake, Armageddon. It could happen.
Or sunshine, love, salvation.

It could, you know. That's why we wake
and look out – no guarantees
in this life.

---

2 Neville Emslie, 2002, *The Minister as Poet*, Dunedin: Knox College.
3 John D. Zizioulas, 2006, *Communion and Otherness*, London: T&T Clark, p. 299.
4 William Stafford, 'Yes', in *The Way It Is*, 1998, Saint Paul, MN: Graywolf Press, p. 247.

But some bonuses, like morning,
like right now, like noon,
like evening.

All artists suffer with loss of confidence at some point in their life, often related to how their work is perceived by observers. Theologically we may relate this to the prophet without honour, the rejections of Jeremiah and Jesus, examples of prophets unheard, unreceived and unattended. F. Scott Fitzgerald had experienced huge acclaim in the 1920s, but in his mid-30s he was in deep debt and very low. He said, 'A writer like me must have an utter confidence, an utter faith in his star. It's an almost mystical feeling, a feeling of nothing-can-happen-to me, nothing-can-touch-me . . . I once had it. But through a series of blows, many of them my own fault, something happened to that sense of immunity and I lost my grip.' The opening night of Puccini's *Madama Butterfly* was a disaster. The audience hissed and yelled at the actors, and the opera closed after one night. Puccini wrote to the distressed leading lady, 'I am sure that this horrible impression will soon be wiped out of our minds . . . with warm affection and confidence in the future, I wish you good luck.' He spent the next few months rewriting the opera, and at its next performance it was a huge success, with numerous encores, and Puccini was called on stage ten times.

A minister, however, cannot rewrite the script so easily. The minister's 'work' is not exhibited or performed for entertainment. Yet with the artist the minister seeks to describe human existence – its condition and its confidence (*con-fidere*, to trust) in itself.

Whence confidence? In ministry the paradigm is relationship, with God, others and self. However, these relationships are fraught which means ministerial confidence is complex in its stability and is affectively poignant. The various relational webs in which the minister is enmeshed can both build and sap confidence in one's faith and vocation.

Whence, then, confidence in calling? Matthew 13 provides some clues.

Biblical reflection

The Sower is the first substantive parable in the Synoptic Gospels and, with its interpretation, is foundational for understanding parables and the kingdom. Snodgrass calls it *the* parable about parables.[5] In Matthew 13,

---

5 Klyne R. Snodgrass, 2008, *Stories with Intent*, Grand Rapids: Eerdmans, p. 145.

the sower casts his seed democratically, for it falls impartially on the path, on rocky ground, among thorns and on good soil. Painters have often portrayed a man with a seed-bag across his hip and his bronzed arm sweeping seed across the variegated landscape. The parable indicates that the word of the kingdom is liberally offered, but how will it be received, and what will be its yield? The next parable concerns a man who sows seed in his field but the crop is contaminated by an enemy who comes at night and sows weeds therein (13.24–30). The master tells his servants they will have to cope with evil even though the kingdom has come, but all will be attended to at the consummation.

Both of these parables picture a man, a field and much seed. The next parable shifts gear and speaks more directly to our subject of confidence in our calling: 'the kingdom of heaven is like a mustard seed that someone took and sowed in his field' (13.31). This scene is more difficult to paint, for it has a man and a field but only one seed, and a tiny one at that. It is an incongruous sight; a man goes into his field to plant a single grain. The sower had cast many thousands of seeds in his field, the master had filled his field with wheat seed, but here a man sows a solitary seed in a barren field.

The kingdom of heaven is like this, says Jesus. What confidence this man has in one seed. He trusts that this solitary, tiny, so thoroughly inauspicious dot of a thing will grow, and grow, and become magnificent, and be such that even other creatures will make nests in its branches. The man has such confidence in the germinating potential and power of this miniscule seed. Further, he has released it. He has let it go and walked away, so allowing it to be vulnerable to bird, insect, drought and the hoof of a passing behemoth. If this seed could feel, and talk, what would it say? 'Help!' or something rather stronger: 'While I was in the hand of the man I was warm and safe and nothing was required of me. But he's left me in the middle of an enormous field! Help, dammit! I'm cold. I'm hot. I'm wet. I'm dry. I'm alone. I'm in danger. He's left me!'

This is what the kingdom of heaven is like. God trusts and entrusts. The parable has been interpreted as the kingdom, inaugurated by Jesus, a solitary man who derives from an inauspicious place, has spread to become like a great tree. However, the meaning of the parable has even wider theological and anthropological claims. The reign of God is like God bending to plant something insubstantial and trusting that it will grow, and grow well:

The Word of God is source and seed;
it comes to die and sprout and grow.

So make your dark earth welcome warm;
root deep the grain God bent to sow.[6]

Ministers can be intimidated by the large field in which they are planted, the paucity of their own gifts, the inclement climate in which they work. We can feel like the solitary seed, aloneness grips the heart and the ministry setting can strangle confidence. But the kingdom of heaven is all about a God who trusts and entrusts. This God is confident in the seed he has planted. This God is confident in the field she has prepared. The mustard seed merely does what it does. It is designed, or 'called', to be planted, and to settle into its surroundings, and to partake of the available nutrients, and to take root, and to grow a stem, then branches, and to stretch and be strong so that other creatures will benefit from it simply being what it is called to be.

This parable teaches us that confidence is derivative. As the farmer has confidence in the mustard seed, so the seed grows in the confidence of the farmer. Likewise for ministry; Jesus the Christ has confidence in his ministers, so we minister in his confidence. Time and again in the Gospel according to Matthew, Jesus shows confidence in those whom he calls. In Matthew 9.35–38, he observes with compassion the 'harassed and help-less' crowds 'like sheep without a shepherd', and he says to his disciples, 'the harvest is plentiful, but the labourers are few; therefore ask the Lord of the harvest to send out labourers into his harvest'. Without waiting for their prayers he immediately summons the disciples and authorizes them to cast out unclean spirits and to cure every disease and sickness (10.1). They are to go unencumbered by money, bag or extra clothes, for they are to preach that the kingdom of heaven has come near, and to heal, raise the dead and cast out demons.

The disciples are told quite specifically in what their confidence is to lie. It is not in things. What they have is Jesus' authority. In our time one of the ways the Church recognizes, and releases, the authority of Jesus is in ordination. The ordained person is recognized as a disciple of Jesus who is gifted to minister, and is authorized by the body of Christ to minister, in the authority of the name and presence of Jesus the Christ. The ordained person is thus 'set apart' – like the mustard seed in the field – to be that which the Farmer orders it to be. The ordained person will be like the solitary seed in the field of the parish, or chaplaincy setting, or vocational environ, but this person must recognize the confidence that the Farmer has in him or her to be that which the Farmer calls this person to be.

---

6 Delores Dufner, 1983, 'The Word of God is Source and Seed', OSB Copyright © 1983, 2003 by GIA Publications, Inc. used by permission.

A more British metaphor is the oak. The kingdom of heaven is like Vice-Admiral Collingwood who walks in the vales of Northumberland, and takes an acorn, drops it on the ground, and presses it into the earth with his shoe. In 200 years, this mighty oak will be cut down, and ships built with its great timber, and the kingdom's fleet will control the oceans of the earth. The kingdom of heaven is like this Vice-Admiral's confidence in the destiny of that which he plants. The acorn will become a glorious tree, for a mighty task, despite its insignificant beginnings. Genetically the acorn and the tree are identical, but the tree does not stand for the Church glorious. The point of the parable is not the outcome but the dynamic. The kingdom of God is not the result of the life, but the life of itself. The Church militant looks for souls saved, and evil rolled back, and overflowing churches. The kingdom, however, is a work, a life, a dynamic, an energy, a metaphysic that can only be experienced and can never be counted. It is qualitative rather than quantitative for it works with little and few in number, but it is life-giving and life-forming in relationship. In this ministers are called and for this they serve. Their confidence is in the God-who-calls, who, ironically, does so by letting us go, planting us like a mustard seed in a large field, like an acorn in a rural vale.

Whence confidence in calling? In the God who bends to press the solitary seed into the large field, in the God whose foot treads the acorn into the grassy vale, in the God who releases us into a strange and lonely place and says, 'You are of the kingdom. Grow!'

Having heard this word will the seed, the acorn, the new minister grow, spreading branches and arms to gather and harbour and nurture life? Or will a consciousness of isolation and a loss of confidence in the Farmer's confidence stymie the call?

Case study

Rachel completed a first-class theology degree before entering theological college where she met James. They discovered a mutual love of walking and social justice issues. By the end of the second year at college they were engaged, then married in the year following ordination as deacons. In due course Rachel completed her Master's in Kierkegaard and occasionally managed to have articles published in good journals. James, an extravert whose early life was spent in sales and marketing, really enjoyed and excelled at the organizational and administrative side of ministry. Rachel gave birth to their first child while a curate and a second child followed a few years later. She was able to juggle the pregnancies, birth, then breastfeeding and care with her studies and writing, which she generally did late at night.

In the final year of their curacies they applied for two posts, an incumbency and NSM of a rural benefice of two parishes that each had two churches. James's extraverted nature proved popular at the interview. Rachel, holding the baby, was not asked many questions, and it was assumed at the outset that James would be the incumbent and Rachel the NSM. It was only during the interviews that Rachel realized the possibility of her being the incumbent and James the NSM. She frowned at herself, bit her lip, but said nothing.

They settled into rural life, James busy in the parish and spending a lot of time reorganizing various rosters, groups and teams. After some years, Rachel decided to accept a part-time post in the diocesan ministry training course training OLMs and Readers. It meant, however, she saw less of James, and she gradually came to realize that she had no one in her life that shared her interests in the outdoors or theology. She began to wonder how different her life might have been had she made more use of her academic qualifications and shared more evenly with James the child-rearing and domestic side of her married life.

Increasingly she found church difficult to stomach, especially the political and institutional dynamics, and yet she knew no greater moment than to stand in the midst of the people of God and together celebrate the Mass, to bring the cure of souls consciously into the presence of God, and join all with the worship of the angels and archangels. Sometimes she wished for ease's sake that she could be unordained, and speak with her own voice, without the label of priesthood.

Recently they went on a family holiday with her in-laws and passed the place where she became able to accept a vocation to the priesthood. Rachel remembered sitting in the Minster and deeply knowing that, whatever any board or committee would say, her vocation was to ordination. Those places in her life, those moments of confidence, extraordinary moments in the most ordinary places, remained important markers in her pilgrimage. Though often she felt adrift, a soul merely wandering to and fro upon the earth, it was these memories that sustained her present being.

At the moment she saw herself as a priest without particular purpose, hanging around and filling in the gaps in other people's rotas, offering ideas that were usually ignored, and she wondered why she went through all the selection, the training, and the agonies of struggle with theology. Recently Rachel reviewed a book for a journal about confidence in the gospel which was littered with stories of the encounters which individuals have recounted of God at work in the world and in their lives. Though good stories, she reflected that none of them spoke of faith when God seemed absent.

Rather than letting it get on top of her she resolved to just get on with the next bit of motherhood, and being the vicar's wife. She acknowledged that those occasional moments of wonder and mystery kept her from going back to the bishop and asking for some ceremony of being made lay. In the moments of greatest doubt she goes on making Eucharist. She stands at the altar leaning on the faith and experience of priests of the past, of the present communion of saints and on the coming kingdom, not in self-confidence but in something much more communal. When asked, she says, 'I am glad that the selection process is about the Church recognizing one's calling, because it is so much bigger than our ebbing and flowing in life.'

Theological reflection

Rachel's dilemma is similar to the mustard seed. Both ask of themselves, 'What in God's name am I doing here?' Interestingly, this question requires attention only when the seed and minister find themselves in an insecure place. Rarely do we attend to personal or ministry formation when life is sweet. Most people in the western world have an innate expectation that life should go quite smoothly, in the main, hence the use of the word 'misfortune' when bad things happen, as if 'fortune' is the standard setting. The mustard seed, or isolated minister, in the large field quakes when the Farmer bends, sows, straightens and walks away. They find it incredibly difficult to believe that this is what the kingdom of heaven is like: to be left alone. The experience is that of aloneness, the observation is that of isolation, the feelings are those of apartness – how is this like the kingdom of heaven?

In the Diocese of Canterbury we recognize the potential of theological reflection and ministerial formation in what we call 'the swampy areas'. Our Ministerial Development Review consists of three parts: the first is 'celebration', to review what has gone well, and to identify that for which one can be thankful; the third is 'development', to identify the personal and ministry areas one will work on in the next period of time, and the resources required for that. The second area is potentially the most fertile, so we call it the 'swampy areas'. These are the experiences of ministry that just have to be endured, the hard yards that are negotiated with grit, prayer, perseverance, and self-control. They can take the form of difficult people, tricky tasks, uncertain deliberations, dis-ease of various kinds and conflictual settings. However, if the minister can step back a little, and become aware of his own responses to these things, and reflect on both the situation and his responses theologically, then exceedingly powerful dynamics come into play. To press the biological metaphor, the seed, out of anxiety, pushes out tendrils which become roots in the earth, and stem and branches into the atmosphere. It finds, in fact, that the Farmer has provided the necessary space to grow to that to which it is genetically predisposed. The relational metaphor has the minister, in isolation, projecting tendrils of doubt and lack of confidence into the substrate and atmosphere in which they are planted, and yet, on reflection, these projections become strong, trunk-like and branch-like, as a result of the environ in which they spread. Critical feedback – friendly and caustic – toughens the bark, thickens the trunk, and strengthens the branch. It can be unpleasant but, by God and dear God, this is a component of ministry. It is not for the fainthearted, the woolly or the person who craves affirmation. Ministry is a crucible that will open up character flaws as few other professions will do, so theological reflection, reflective practice and self-understanding are essential.

Do artists feel confident that they have done what they set out to do? Paul Valéry said that a poem is never finished, only abandoned. Did Michelangelo truly create what he originally perceived when he first looked at the block of marble? The preacher feels the same, and what assignment at college would not have been better with a little more time and a few tweaks here and there? Similarly with the call, one's vocation, the initial promise always has a sense of incompleteness. It is being worked out, rather like salvation, with fear and trembling, and so one's calling is never entire, never completed, nor ever fulfilled. As such, 'confidence' in calling is best expressed soteriologically, for it is both a present experience and that which is to be fulfilled. It is not something we own, but a relationship that is experienced.

The call, then, is to follow and relate and believe. The word 'believe' is too often employed in the modern Church as cognitive assent to theological statements and the creeds are read as lines of truths. In fact 'believe' has always meant 'to trust in' (*life* and *love* come from the same root), so when worshippers utter, 'I believe in God the Father, maker of heaven and earth . . .' they are proclaiming their trust in this particular God. Their life depends on it, so confidence in our calling grows according to the nature of the relationship we have with the One whom we accompany on the journey through life.

Note the paradox. On the one hand the farmer seemingly abandons the seed, confident in its ability to grow and flourish in an apparently difficult environment. The farmer has confidence in the seed to do that which it has been 'called' to do. Likewise Jesus sends out his disciples confident in their training, commitment and stamina. On the other hand, the seed grows in the field prepared by the farmer and in the space cleared by him. Similarly, the minister ministers in God's world, appropriating the resources of the present kingdom, in particular life in the Spirit, and confident in the kingdom to come.

Ministerial reflection

It continually saddens me to hear ordained and lay colleagues speak about the call proprietorially. I understand the intention, for having 'heard' and 'received' it, one wants to acknowledge its claim on one's life for it establishes a new kind of identity and, thus, purpose. However, to speak of 'my' ministry is as immature as speaking of 'my' church, or 'my' people. No payment, no gold, no silver, no copper, no bag, no second tunic, no sandals, no staff, said Jesus (Matt. 10.9–10), and however we duck shove this to interpret it for a particular mission on which Jesus sent his disciples, the fact that Matthew records it for his community indicates something of its intention for discipleship that must live on in later Christian communities. At the very least we are called to travel light, and to possess little as disciples.

> So we put our beginning down in your continuing,
>> confident of the edges of our faith,
>> and so free for the big things now to be
> learned and received and enacted.[7]

Thirty years or so before Matthew penned his Gospel, St Paul had exhorted the believers at Philippi to 'look not to your own interests, but to the interest of others' and urges them to be of the same mind as Christ Jesus who had 'emptied himself, taking the form of a slave' (Phil. 2.4, 7). This theology of kenosis stands in stark contrast to ministers who have a freehold attitude to vocation. It is mine, they say, and the income of prestige, status and power that comes with it. I am struck by the line that soon follows in the hymn, 'being found in human form' (v. 7d). The Greek is literally 'and being found in form as a human being', where the word *heuretheis* from *heuriskō*, 'to find', has a sense of surprise, in that 'in the

---

7 Walter Brueggemann, 2004, from 'On Reading the Old Testament', in *Inscribing the Text*, Minneapolis: Fortress, p. 20.

eyes of those who saw His incarnate life, He was "as a man"'.[8] The passive intensifies the sense of humility on Christ's part for he was found to be a human, rather than came to be Lord of humans. Christ's activity is restricted to self-emptying and human activity is finding the Christ to be, utterly surprisingly, human.

At the conclusion of the initial ministerial education (IME) period the Church of England expects curates' sense of vocation to be 'obedient, realistic and informed'. We have argued that 'our' call is derivative for we find the nature of this call in the example of Christ. As people found Christ Jesus to be human, the call we experience is found, and validated, by others too, and in this lies our confidence. The Church ordains those in whom it has confidence, in that it finds, or recognizes, such a person to be ordered in their life and commitment to Christ Jesus. Obedience is to Christ, but to the Christ whom each of us must 'find' to be the One who emptied himself to be human. In other words ministry has a central Christological task of discovery. We are continually struck by the ongoing discovery that Christ is human and we find his humanity in surprising ways and in surprising people and in surprising settings. Having found that, will we be obedient to the Christ who calls us to participate with him in these places?

True discovery involves a good deal of boundary-riding, pushing beyond the previous comfort zones. I know a training incumbent whose first words to the deacon are, 'This is a time for you to take risks. If things go well, you get the kudos, if they go pear-shaped, then I pick up the pieces.' This incumbent recognizes that the curacy period is an opportunity for discovery of the deep self and discovery of the depths of Christ. Finding out who Christ is and what he is about will always have a degree of discomfort, and sometimes the degree is significant. We will be led into places that will be uncomfortable, but the difficulty lies not so much in the setting – poverty, danger, exposure of vulnerabilities – but in the discovery of what Christ is like in these places. We find that Christ loves people we do not, Christ welcomes people we exclude, and Christ touches people we dare not go near. This, more than anything else, tests our confidence. The very One who calls tests our call like no one else. 'Do you love me?' he asks John, three times.

There is a moving scene in Zeffirelli's film *Jesus of Nazareth* where Jesus enters Levi's house following an argument in Peter's home. A party is in full swing and Jesus comes among Levi's friends: tax collectors, reprobates and 'sinners' scoffing, boozing, and lying all over each other. The disciples, standing outside, are aghast at Jesus entering Levi's home with

---

8 Ralph P. Martin, *Carmen Christi*, Cambridge: Cambridge University Press, 1967, p. 207.

these people. Eventually Peter joins them and Jesus tells a story which we know as the prodigal son. All stop to listen, Levi's friends inside, and the disciples outside. At the conclusion of the story Simon Peter, recognizing he is the elder son, comes in, asks for forgiveness, and places his hand of acceptance on Levi.

The dramatic setting vividly captures what it means to be called. All hear, but those who follow are generally required to move from comfort to discomfort, yet they find a capacity to do so when they realize that Jesus himself is already there, and when they realize that they themselves need to be emptied of previous orientations to security, Jesus calls. In him and towards him is our confidence.

Thus, when we speak about 'confidence in calling' it is with a prayer for the inner life to be more kind, gentle, compassionate and empathic, and that the outer life may have strength of character, integrity and purpose. A senior policeman taught me once his prayer for his work, and I think it is apt for ministers too – 'Lord, give me a softer belly and a stronger backbone.' Our confidence is in the God-who-calls, not in the calling of itself. The call is not something we have, it has no deed of title, for it is a life born every day, and in every post, and in every setting.

2

Making Friends

PAUL BAYES

Anyone who begins ordained life needs to handle with particular skill the distinction between the role and the person who inhabits it. We minister in a Church that sees itself, among other things, as a loving community of friends. At the same time we minister in a culture where great clarity of professional role is expected, demanded and valued.

Augustine of Hippo famously said 'With you I am a Christian, for you I am a bishop.'[1] With the Church a member of the community, for the Church a bishop, a priest, a deacon. With the Church a Christian friend, for the Church a Christian minister.

How will these tensions be handled by the newly ordained and those who mentor and accompany them? If the Christian Church is in any sense a community of friends, what does this mean for its ministers? Is the human warmth of the priest central in a church built on the Incarnation? Or is it rather, 'professionally speaking', that human warmth is optional, or even counter-productive? Does the manifest humanity of the minister reveal the truth of God or conceal it? In short can the local congregation be at the same time a community of friends and a collection of clients?

Everyone will answer these questions through the way they choose to live, and perhaps in their reaction to the way Jesus chose to live.

A friend of mine

'This is my command, that you love each other, in just that way that I have loved you. Nobody has any bigger love than this, that somebody lays their life down on behalf of the friends of theirs. You are friends of mine whenever you do the things I command you. No more do I call you servants, because the servant does not know at all what his master is doing; but I have now called you friends, because all things that I heard from my Father I have made known to you.' (John 15.12–15, my translation)

---

1 The idea is in *Sermon 46*, among other places.

Thus the LORD used to speak to Moses face to face, as one speaks to a friend. (Exod. 33.11)

Why do people say 'a friend of mine'? You never hear anyone say, 'Oh, Andy Rackstraw is a very good plumber of mine.' 'Dr Jones, an experienced anaesthetist of mine.' 'Rowan Williams, the bearded Archbishop of mine.'

Friendship commits. It is powerful and not easily broken. 'Rackstraw was my plumber, but he specializes in commercial pipe work now.' 'Jones was my anaesthetist, but now she's on maternity leave.' 'Williams was my Archbishop, but now I live in Glasgow.' No one is demeaned or threatened by these changes. But 'You used to be a friend of mine, but not any more'? This says something very personal about you, and about me, and about our future.

Joiners make tables. Lovers make love. What do friends make? Well, nothing. They make friends. Friendship commits and binds, but it is also gratuitous, playful, unproductive. It is an end, not a means.

Prophetic friendship

Among much else, the Church is a community that makes friends. And in English culture a friendly church communicates the truth of God in a way that is both vulgar and prophetic.

When the sharing of the Peace was introduced into the Anglican Eucharist in England, it became contentious. The aim was to make Christian community manifest; but not everyone sees the absence of manifest community as a problem. The socially mobile, the self-sufficient, and the wealthy in particular tend not to miss it. In that climate the enthusiastic sharing of the Peace was seen as a physical symptom of a church that was looking too hard for friendship. Informally a coalition grew to oppose it. This had various strands. They included emotionally inhibited Englishmen and Englishwomen ('Have we been introduced?' 'Do I know you?' 'I'm a refugee from the kiss of peace!') and those whose theology had no room for the human community ('It's just me and my Maker, Vicar!').

Together with these there were, and are, a good number of people afraid that a cheap togetherness devalues the faith. They see it as particularly cheap when it involves the clergy: 'In a sense, the more shy and retiring we are, the better. Nothing is more tiresome than the gregarious young priest who overwhelms his parishioners with "friendship", slaps people on the back and asks them to call him "Tom". . .'[2]

---

2 Kenneth Child, 1970, *In His Own Parish*, London: SPCK, p. 15.

And preferment does not get 'Tom' off the hook. Monica Furlong grumbles about 'a habit of speaking about a bishop in conversation by his title and Christian name – Bishop Tom, Bishop Jim, Bishop Timothy . . . I fear what it indicates is a willed intimacy, a pretence that bishop, clergy and laity are on much closer terms than they actually are. It is not very convincing.'[3]

From this perspective our faith has become a source of mockery precisely at the point of friendship and community. Toes curl at the very thought of worshipping believers being friendly and smiling, let alone hugging with all the dangers of blurred boundaries that brings. A church seeking to be friendly is seen to be a church that has embraced foolishness, that has lost its way.

Meanwhile with unusual fortitude and consistency, in the teeth of all this opposition from the socially comfortable, a large part of the Church of Jesus Christ keeps on trying to be friendly.

The local church normally limps. It will normally contain disproportionate numbers of lonely people, of the elderly poor ('When someone shakes my hand at church, it's the only time in the week anyone touches me'), of lone parents, younger children, those with learning disability, and those who choose community not because it is cosy, but because Jesus promised that he would be found there. For these people friendliness is not an optional extra. It is a prophetic act, valued most by those who need it most. Like all prophecy, the friendliness of the church confronts. It demands a decision.

And yet. 'Such a friendly church.' When you hear this inside a church building, it is not usually said as an insult but as a compliment. It does not simply mean that the church is full of people who are friends of one another. If you are new, that can be the mark of a most unfriendly church. For a stranger to describe a community as friendly means that friendship has been offered to them, openly. When it is openly offered, friendship is recognized for what it is. It is not normally refused.

Open friendship

'The son of man has come eating and drinking, and you say, Look, a man, a glutton, a drunk, a friend of taxmen and sinners' (Luke 7.34, my translation).

Winston Churchill liked pigs. When asked why, he replied, 'Cats look down on you as your superiors. Dogs look up to you like your servants. But a pig will treat you as an equal.'

---

3 Monica Furlong, 2000, *C of E: The State It's In*, London: Hodder and Stoughton, p. 252.

The German theologian Jürgen Moltmann would have seen the point of this: 'One does not have to submit to a friend. One neither looks up to nor down at a friend. One can look a friend in the face.'[4]

For Moltmann 'open friendship' describes the Church's way of relating. Friendship is for him the right word to describe Jesus' relationship with us, because it is so unpretentious. '"Friend" is not a functional title, nor a designation of office, nor a role one is expected to play in society . . . If friendship is not these things, what is it? It is a personal relation, "someone who likes you", someone you like . . .'[5]

Friends open up to one another free space for free life.[6]

Perhaps this freedom is the natural mark of the community of Jesus, who said that we were to know the truth, and that the truth would set us free. In English and in Moltmann's German, the word 'friend' is rooted in older words which mean 'free one'. 'There is no longer Jew or Greek, there is no longer slave or free, there is no longer male and female; for all of you are one in Christ Jesus' (Gal. 3.28).

If we are indeed one, what is our relationship to be? Friendship. 'The friend is the new person, the true person, the free person, the person who likes to be with other people.'[7]

Finally, Moltmann sketches what a church of friendship would look like:

What would it be like if Christian congregations and communities were no longer to regard themselves only as 'the community of saints' or as 'the congregation of the faithful' but as such a 'community of friends'? . . . Then they would have to assemble in grass roots communities that would live close to the people and with the people in the friendship of Jesus.[8]

Carlo Carretto, saying the same thing, sees it as rooted in Scripture:

Today's people . . . want a Church made of friendship, of genuine contacts, of mutual interchange of little things. But more than anything else, a Church that feeds them with the Word, a Church that works with them by physically taking them by the hand, a Church whose face

4 Jürgen Moltmann, 1978, *The Open Church*, London: SCM Press, p. 51.
5 Moltmann, *The Open Church*, p. 51.
6 Moltmann, *The Open Church*, p. 52.
7 Moltmann, *The Open Church*, p. 53.
8 Moltmann, *The Open Church*, p. 62.

is like that of the Church of Luke, of Mark, of John, a Church that is just starting – that smells of beginnings.[9]

'A church that is just starting'. Carretto is thinking of Jesus' group.

Jesus was born and grew to manhood in the community of a family in a village. He travelled to Jerusalem as one of a group of travellers, and visited the temple there as a boy so that he could be in the midst of a group of teachers.

He stood in the midst of John's community at his baptism. He was transfigured in the presence of three of his friends. He was crucified as one of three criminals. At the foot of his cross stood the fragments of his community. A group of people cared for his body after his death.

After his resurrection, he walked to Emmaus as one of three. In the Upper Room, he breathed his Spirit on his group. At the lakeside, he prepared breakfast for his friends. On the mountain, while he was giving a group his blessing, he parted from them.

Between these events, for three and a half years, he engaged in his ministry.

'Very truly, I tell you, we speak of what we know and testify to what we have seen' (John 3.11). Jesus' ministry was full of variety and incident. He preached publicly to thousands and fed them. He ministered God's healing to all those who asked him, and a few more besides. He and his disciples wore themselves out in the pastoral care of the crowds. He also spent a great deal of time alone with his Father, in prayer and reflection.

But the Gospels show one overwhelming priority. They say that the main thing Jesus did with his time was to choose a group of people and to spend time with them. Almost exactly half of St Mark's Gospel is devoted to time spent by Jesus with his disciples.

'He went up the mountain and called to him those whom he wanted, and they came to him. And he appointed twelve, whom he also named apostles, to be with him, and to be sent out to proclaim the message' (Mark 3.13–14). Jesus invested his life in his group. From among them he chose twelve to say something symbolic about Israel, but these twelve were not headhunted to do a job. Eventually they were indeed sent out, apostles, to proclaim the message; but the first reason Jesus chose them was 'so that they might be with him'.

So the priority of Jesus' ministry, and the context of Jesus' teaching, is the common life of a group of friends. It is not exclusive. There is no qualification for entry. But it is not cheap. When its door is opened to

9 Carlo Carretto, 1984, *I Sought and I Found*, London: Darton, Longman and Todd, p. 34.

others, they do not always step in: 'When Jesus heard this, he said to him, "There is still one thing lacking. Sell all that you own and distribute the money to the poor, and you will have treasure in heaven; then come, follow me." But when he heard this, he became sad; for he was very rich' (Luke 18.22–23).

What happened in this group? Life happened. The life of the disciples, their meals, their jealousies and squabbles, their parties, their travels, their worries about sick relatives, their work, their shared hopes, the demands made on them. This life was not 'religious life'. It was their common life. Although the disciples asked Jesus to teach them to pray, there is no evidence that they constituted a prayer group. Their life was meat and potatoes, daily bread, not sherry (or coffee, or doughnuts) after a service.

And Jesus invested his life in all of this. The shared life became the medium of the gospel message. From the very beginning it was, as Lesslie Newbigin said: 'The only hermeneutic of the gospel is a community that lives by it.'[10] Adolf von Harnack made the same point over a century ago: 'It was *koinonia*, and not any evangelist, which proved to be the most effective missionary.'[11]

How far does today's Church, and the approach of its ordained ministers, fit with such a picture of human yieldedness?

Warmth and friendship

Not the cry but the flight of the wild duck leads the flock to fly and to follow.[12]

Warmth is what is valued above all.[13]

Robert Runcie when Principal of Cuddesdon College spoke of 'the sociability required of a priest'. To *require* sociability seems a bit strong, especially in a church most of whose priests are introverts. And yet it's possible to see human warmth as the fruit of character, as demonstrating faith, and as a bedrock skill for mission and evangelism.

The national Weddings Project invited its secular research partners to interview 822 people, in order to discover what their church wedding

10 Lesslie Newbigin, 1989, *The Gospel in a Plural Society*, London: SPCK, p. 227.

11 Adolf von Harnack, 1908, *The Mission and Expansion of Christianity*, London: James Moffatt, p. 145.

12 Chinese proverb. Quoted by John Adair, 2002, *Effective Strategic Leadership*, Basingstoke: Macmillan, p. 61.

13 Unpublished research commissioned by the Archbishops' Council and conducted by Futureal, for the national Weddings Project in 2009.

journey had meant to them. The results emphasized the central importance of the vicar to the unchurched, and the extraordinary extent to which simple human warmth in vicars was valued and was used by God to mediate grace and welcome to those on and beyond the Church's threshold. Thirty years ago in *Finding Faith Today* John Finney confirmed the same fact. For him, the 'affability' of the priest was a crucial factor in the growth of the Church.[14]

This requirement of sociability demands balance and poise in the ordained; but not as an inbuilt disposition, nor as a skill-set. It is more a matter of *askesis*; a discipline of the spirit rooted in genuine self-acceptance as a life choice.

Friendship needs no superstars. God's chosen ones are often broken people – Abraham, David, Peter, Paul. We know that God brings strength and healing to others out of the wounds and the brokenness of his ministers.

But John Finney is surely right when he says:

> Those who have a right regard for themselves and their ministry are able to be outgoing and relaxed . . . This implies an emotional freedom . . . if leaders are personally cold and aloof, it is not surprising that they preach a Christianity which is uninteresting, uninspiring and unchallenging.[15]

And when he goes on to speak of leaders who may lack this inner security:

> Such leaders will appear 'twitchy' and uncertain in personal relationships. Colin Urquhart tells how people in his church used to say to him, 'Colin, we do not know you', and how he would say to himself, 'Good' . . . We build a wall of protection and hide behind it from the real or pretended attacks of others. It may be more comfortable, but we are not following the One who was prepared to be vulnerable to all, even his enemies.[16]

The Baptist theologian Michael Walker sees to the root:

> Our view of God can be fundamental to the quality of our human relationships . . . The Christian church today is full of cries for God's

---

14 John Finney, 1992, *Finding Faith Today*, London: Bible Society, pp. 51–9.

15 John Finney, 1989, *Understanding Leadership*, London: Darton, Longman and Todd, p. 66.

16 Finney, *Understanding Leadership*, p. 66.

power. We want to be powerful and do not always see what power does to other people. If we are uncertain of his love for us then our human relationships will have about them a tentative and cautious quality.[17]

Servants and friends

Ordained life is impossible without . . . deep love for the health of the church.[18]

'Servant leadership' is a good phrase, one that can point to a vital truth. In practice, it can be a liberation, or a paradox, or a contradiction, and sometimes simply a fraud disguising power games. Maybe this is one reason why Jesus called his disciples servants no longer.

A rabbi, a cantor and a synagogue cleaner are praying. The rabbi says, 'Look at me, Lord, I'm nothing!' The cantor says, 'Look at me, Lord, I'm nothing!' The cleaner says, 'Look at me, Lord, I'm nothing!' The rabbi whispers to the cantor, nodding towards the cleaner: 'Who is he, to say that he's nothing?'

Servants can really be in charge. Jean Genet's play *The Maids* explores this with savage humour. Joseph Losey's film *The Servant*, scripted by Harold Pinter, offers a pitiless view of the same matter. In the Harry Potter books we are introduced to the house-elves with their relentless insistence on spending their lives in service. It is an inspiring vision – or is it? Hermione Grainger doesn't think so and, in the end, neither do we. Service, like everything else, is made to be shared. It's greedy to hoard it.

From time to time, Marie Antoinette pretended to be a shepherdess for fun, while always remaining royal – a shepherdess with a golden crook. They may look good, even in church, but golden crooks are good for nothing. Stop pretending, your majesty. If you want a stick made of gold, buy a sceptre.

Professional friends, professional strangers

In Hebrew thought the opposite of friend is not enemy but stranger.[19]

Christ in mouth of friend and stranger.[20]

17 Michael Walker, 1986, 'Human and Spiritual Development', in *Spirituality and Human Wholeness*, London: British Council of Churches, p. 64.

18 Christopher Cocksworth and Rosalind Brown, 2002, *Being a Priest Today*, Norwich: Canterbury Press, p. 33.

19 Sallie McFague, in Elisabeth Moltmann-Wendel, 2000, *Rediscovering Friendship*, London: SCM Press, p. 9.

20 St Patrick's Breastplate.

Much ministerial formation is concerned with the value of emotional distance in the Church. Those who defend the role-distance of the ordained genuinely see it as a form of love.

Snowy has lived and worked in south-east London as a community worker for the last 20 years. During that time he has become widely known and respected in the community. Recently he was ordained. One evening a man who lives locally but is not a churchgoer cornered him in a pub and wanted to know what to do about his marriage, which was on the rocks. 'Can I have a word with you, vicar?', he asked. He knew Snowy's name and had often had a drink with him before. Yet this time he addressed him as 'vicar'. The man was looking to Snowy for help with three expectations: first, for someone who could help him with access to resource from God; second, for an official church person (not just a Christian); and third, for someone who was trustworthy, authoritative. What he needed at that moment was not Snowy the friend but Snowy the vicar.[21]

More and more ours is a society served by professionals. Professional competence is valued and has become the benchmark for ministerial life. Skill-sets are measurable, and the transgressing of boundaries is rightly seen as a disaster for ministry and often for personal holiness too. People who don't know how to police the boundaries of their persona are a menace indeed.

And yet the ministry of professionals is a stranger to friendship. People know that, and they often do not like it.

- In the late 1980s, I visited a bereaved family in a street of terraced houses. The elderly widow was chiefly saddened by one thing. 'In the past Mrs so-and-so down the road would have come in and laid out his body. We would have all helped. But Mrs so-and-so isn't with us any more. Now he's just been spirited away by that bloody undertaker.'
- In Bradford, where I was born, the stand in the local football ground burned down on 11th May 1985. Fifty-two people died, and many others were injured. The community was traumatized. The TV news that night told us that a coach load of bereavement counsellors had been summoned and was now available for anyone who needed help. Many in the town resented this. 'Don't they think we can help each other, then?' one of our neighbours said angrily.

Frankfurt is the twin town of Birmingham. In 1975, I was invited as a representative of Birmingham Samaritans to visit the 'Telefonseelsorge',

---

21 Wesley Carr (ed.), 1992, *Say One For Me*, London: SPCK, p. 40.

the church-run telephone counselling services, in Frankfurt. Because of
state funding for church work, these are fully staffed by professional social workers, and not by volunteers, as with the Samaritans here. German
Christian leaders were frankly astonished that we would entrust the care
of the suicidal to a bunch of amateurs. Didn't we want to see the job well
done? But in England the Samaritans were overstretched by high demand.
And in Germany they were cutting down the Telefonseelsorge, because
there wasn't enough for them to do. How do the Samaritans describe
what they do? They call it 'befriending'.

Nothing personal

'Tell Mike it was nothing personal', said Tessio. 'I always liked him.'
'He understands that,' said Hagan.[22]

Writing in the 1960s, G. R. Dunstan speaks of 'role morality'. It means
that a professional has the duty to suppress his or her personality in order
to do the job better. 'Let him be as much a man as he will, as full a man,
as bizarre a man, as much a "character", as much a "personality" – and
the more the better – yet his professional conduct will be that of a priest –
detached . . . from purely personal idiosyncrasy.'[23]

For me this sort of thinking has diminished the particular contribution
that the Church can make to the world in which it is set. The transforming
power of role-in-friendship has been replaced by a battery of skills, designed
to keep the clergy safe as they make their way through the thick jungles of
transference, of projection, and of dependency on the part of their 'clients'.

Many of the books that ordinands are asked to read will advise them,
for their own survival, to ensure that they have a network of friends outside the parish. Indeed for most of these books the only place to have
friends is outside the parish. Certainly this was the mood when I was
trained for ministry. It was made clear that we would not be useful to our
parishes or to our congregations unless we could hold our distance. In the
1960s, Graham Pulkingham found the same:

There was never a whisper [about such things as knowing and being
known] during my own generation of pastoral training. In fact NOT
to be known by the flock was subtly held forth as a good professional

---

22 Mario Puzo, *The Godfather*.
23 G. R. Dunstan (ed.), 1970, *The Sacred Ministry*, London: SPCK, p. 4.

stance for pastors; burdensome personal problems could be dealt with 'under the stole' or in professional therapeutic sessions.[24]

The training and preparation of the clergy has many good aims, including that they should be able to survive their ministry. 'He said to them, "Come away to a deserted place all by yourselves and rest a while." For many were coming and going, and they had no leisure even to eat. And they went away in the boat to a deserted place by themselves' (Mark 6.31).

The ordained meet many people who demand things from them – answers, certainty, services, money. This can be exhausting. It is not good for any Christian to burn out, seeking to be and to do for others what only God can be or do for them. And so it is absolutely right and proper to teach ministers how to defend themselves against burnout.

However, survival-thinking can skew ministry in a particular professional direction. It's possible to build a system of caring entirely around emotional distance. This has been done. However, it is not ordained Christian ministry, but psychoanalysis.

D. W. Winnicott spelled out Freud's own method. As part of the description he said this: 'Freud . . . showed love for the patient by giving him time, reliability, dependability. He showed hate for the patient by restricting the time and in the matter of the fee.'[25]

Freudian psychoanalysis takes emotional distance to its limit. Classical analytic training insists that the therapist must be emotionally 'abstinent'. The blander and less idiosyncratic the analyst, the more intense and stormy will be the transference, as the patient projects all his or her unresolved relationships onto this clear, unmarked screen.

To minister properly like this is pretty costly.

A patient enters the consulting room and lies down on the couch. Her mother has died. She tells the analyst this. The analyst expresses absolutely no response. After a few moments' silence the analyst says 'You're resisting something.' The patient gets up and quits the analysis, telling the analyst 'You're sicker than I am.'

But when the analyst is supervised, he is found to have done the right thing. Only by being unresponsive, his supervisor says, could he have given the patient a chance to say something about the death of her mother – perhaps that she was secretly pleased to see the back of her. Perhaps if

24 W. Graham Pulkingham, 1980, 'To Know and Be Known', in *Renewal: an Emerging Pattern*, Poole: Celebration Publishing, p. 162.

25 In Janet Malcolm, 1980, *Psychoanalysis: The Impossible Profession*, London: Picador, p. 43.

the analyst had expressed sympathy, this opportunity would have been lost.[26]

All this can work. And yet the history of analysis is the history of break-away, heretical schools, in almost every case founded by intuitive healers – Jung, Ferenczi, Perls – who could no longer put up with the purity of this way of helping people. Professional therapy with its absolute structure of role-boundary is a poor model for the parish priest. The boundaries between therapist and patient have to be ruthlessly clear. Only so can they play with fire and not be burned. But if the minister is to know and be known, then she or he must put Freud's box of matches down.

Still, many of the ordained have chosen to bind to themselves the distance of the clergy role. They then live that role in the parish as their preferred way of being. As with Marcel Marceau in his famous mime, their mask welds to their face. It stays on for life, for better or worse.

Some clergy choose to live this way. If they do, then they pay a price. They are led into an habitual and almost unbreakable distancing from the members of the Christian community within which they are called to live.

There is no doubt that, both through their choice and despite their choice, God will bless their ministry. But projection works both ways. Choosing distance in order to work with the transference in their pastoral relationships, they will face the pressures of perfection, and they will need constant and sustained supervision in order not to collude with it.

Transparency

Using a striking and compelling image Benjamin Gordon-Taylor has said: 'The priest is ultimately called to be transparent, but usefully so, like a pair of glasses.'[27]

I think I know what he means, but I disagree. For me the priest/leader is called to be transparent, simply so, not a lens, but clear glass. It is God's use of this transparency that is the glory of the Church. 'The street of the city is pure gold, transparent as glass. I saw no temple in the city, for its temple is the Lord God the Almighty and the Lamb' (Rev. 21.21–22).

To be transparent or vulnerable is hard. It takes courage, but it takes a humdrum courage, involves no skill, and is nothing heroic. The outworking of transparency and vulnerability is unromantic, dull, and probably humiliating to the individual concerned.

---

26 In Malcolm, *Psychoanalysis: The Impossible Profession*, pp. 74–5.

27 Benjamin Gordon-Taylor, in George Guiver (ed.), 2001, *Priests in a People's Church*, London: SPCK, p. 23.

I was privileged to serve as a deacon with a transparent leader. He did not really want to be one. Indeed, he saw himself very much as the priest in role, the father of the church family. But in my sixth week of life as an ordained deacon, his personal life collapsed; his wife left him. On the same night, he conducted a wedding rehearsal with astonishing bravura, rejoicing with those who rejoice. But within the church community he could not keep up such an act. The sense of defeat that his marriage breakdown gave him was compounded by deep, deep shame that (as he saw it) he was letting his people down.

In fact, the church simply pastored him. The Mothers' Union wrote a letter to the bishop – no need to worry, bishop; they would look after him. Love and energy was released in the community, to the great blessing of the church and of the wider society in that town.

I was privileged to serve there, because he was a good trainer and became a friend. With him I was able to learn a key lesson at first hand – that in the community of Jesus talk of shepherds and sheep is mostly useful, but is always provisional and shifting, and is sometimes simply false.

Then after a few months as a curate, inflicting my academic theological notions on a patient and tolerant congregation, I mentioned in passing in a sermon that I had had a nervous breakdown as a student. The feedback was immediate and unsettling. People seemed to think that this illness qualified me to help them. They began to share their own neuroses, and to ask – not 'what do you think I should do?', but 'what did you do?' And the alchemy of friendship began.

The world is full of pain. The needs of even a small human community are for practical purposes unlimited. Human beings do not have the resources to offer God's care to one another or to the world. Only by God's Spirit can this be done, by God's power made perfect in our human weakness.

Priesthood and leadership depend on people relating. If they relate instrumentally, treating each other as 'it', then 'things' will get done. But this would be priesthood and leadership as a stranger to friendship. Alongside that, beneath that, increasingly instead of that, is it possible that we might act with transparency as Jesus did? 'He took with him Peter and the two sons of Zebedee, and began to be grieved and agitated. Then he said to them, "I am deeply grieved, even to death; remain here, and stay awake with me"' (Matt. 26.37–38).

The transparency of Christ is an awesome thing. We want to avoid it. And we normally manage to do so. The only arena in which we cannot avoid it is the same arena in which Jesus experienced it – the arena of committed, honest community. There 'the word is near you, on your lips and in your heart'.

The Church has replaced it with a great many helpful and professional things. But perhaps a pearl of very great price has been lost? Let me end this reflection with Graham Pulkingham's challenge, which spoke to my own broken life. It was given out of his own broken life. It speaks to anyone who seeks to live in a broken, healing, human church:

I now suspect that there is no more effective way to make disciples of Jesus than to gather men and women together, not artificially, but out of the givenness of their life circumstance, into a profound fellowship of godly concern under the charge of open, defenceless, fully 'given' pastoral leaders.[28]

---

28 Pulkingham, *To Know and Be Known*, p. 163.

3

Priestly Formation

ANDREW D. MAYES

What is formation?

'Where did you train for the ministry?' 'What is your training incumbent
like?' The language of training is all-pervasive, but can betray a prag-
matic approach to ministry that is simply skills-based and task-focused.
The language of training can lead to an exhausting, functionalist view of
ministry which emphasizes out of all proportion the competencies needed
in order to accomplish tasks successfully and with maximum results and
greatest efficiency. The language of formation prophetically questions this
approach – it makes us ask what deeper work of God is taking place in
the candidate: it encourages us to discern the transformative work of the
Spirit in us. It prompts us to move from a stress on *doing* to an awareness
of *being*, or at least to hold these two modes within a creative dialectical
tension.

The language of formation resonates with the theme of God's creativity in us. As Ephesians (2.10, JB) puts it: 'we are God's work of art',
God's masterpiece. God is longing to shape and reshape our lives. God
is ever creative. In Genesis, 'the LORD God formed man from the dust of
the ground, and breathed into his nostrils the breath of life; and the man
became a living being' (2.7). Jeremiah 18 gives us the powerful image of
the divine potter who reworks the clay into the beautiful vessel he seeks
to create (cf. Isa. 45.9 and 2 Tim. 2.20–21). Isaiah links formational language to vocation: 'Thus says the LORD, he who created you, O Jacob,
he who formed you, O Israel . . . I have called you by name, you are
mine . . .' (43.1); 'The LORD says, who formed me in the womb to be his
servant . . . I will give you as a light to the nations' (49.5–6).

The language of formation is important to Paul, who is 'in the pain of
childbirth until Christ is formed in you' (Gal. 4.19). Paul longs that we
develop the mind of Christ or the form (*morphe*) of Christ, 'who, though
he was in the form of God . . . emptied himself, taking the form of a slave'
(Phil. 2.6, 7). Paul writes of a radical work of ongoing change: we are not

to be conformed to the world but transformed by the renewal of our minds (Rom. 12.2). The Christian vocation and destiny is 'to be conformed to the image of his Son' (Rom. 8.29). Paul uses the Greek word *summorphosis* to show that growth into Christlikeness involves a dynamic process of being reshaped.

The language of formation, then, points us to an inner work of the Spirit in which our identity in Christ takes shape. In relation to ministerial formation, it is not only a question of the jobs I do but, rather, of the person I am becoming. This is not only about character development but, even more profoundly, about a sense of who we are as Christian ministers. Whatever view of the priesthood may be held, the newly ordained must discover for themselves a new sense of authority and humility, a God-given clarity of self-understanding, an awareness that they are a work in progress, a growing into the new identity celebrated in ordination. The Anglican ordinal suggests the particular way in which the ordained are to seek Christlikeness in their ministries: priests 'are to set the example of the Good Shepherd always before them, as the pattern of their calling'. Deacons are to seek a greater assimilation to the image of Christ the Servant. Thus the minister will experience an increasing *identification* with Christ, an ever-closer *resemblance* to him, becoming a real and faithful *image* of Christ, Shepherd and Servant. This is the heart of priestly formation: developing *relationship* with Christ within the mystery of the Trinity. We can make an analogy with baptism: as in Romans 6 Paul invites the baptized to become what they are, and to live out their baptism, so deacons and priests are invited to become what they are, and realize ever more fully their fundamental identity and being as ministers of Christ, declared in their ordination. As Karl Rahner put it: 'You are only what you should be as a priest, if you bring your whole life into your vocation . . . Your life-work is to establish an ever closer intimacy between yourself and your office.'[1] Priestly formation involves the integration of the office and the person, and the union of the human being with Christ the priest. Of course, this is to be set within the perspective of the collaborative ministry of the whole people of God. Careful attention needs to be given to what is *distinctive* in formation in relation to the different orders of deacon, priest and bishop, and what is common to the discipleship of the whole people of God.

Christ calls his first disciples: 'Follow me and I will make you . . .' (Mark 1.17). Formation is about the interplay between the raw material of our lives and the divine call, as God remoulds us as his vessels and

---

1 K. Rahner, 1968, *Servants of the Lord*, Tunbridge Wells: Burns and Oates.

instruments. This is not to suggest that we are passive clay: we are rather invited into a synergy with God, and training ministers and spiritual directors will help us to identify any human resistances to this divine work, as well as opportunities which open us more fully to the formational process. Formation is both gift and call, grace and task, divine initiative and human response: 'work out your own salvation, for it is God who is at work in you' (Phil. 2.12–13). We can hinder or advance God's work of formation in us. We need to take responsibility for our own formation. Let us explore four aspects of formation, concluding each with its challenge to our practice of ministry.

Formed by the word

'All scripture is inspired by God and can profitably be used for teaching, for refuting error, for guiding people's lives and teaching them to be holy. This is how the man who is dedicated to God becomes fully equipped and ready for any good work' (2 Tim. 3.16, JB). In this passage, four reasons are given for the Scripture, and reading this we could ask, with Timothy, four questions of our ministry:

- What am I learning right now from God's Word?
- What weaknesses in my life does it speak to?
- How do I allow God's Word to guide me?
- What am I learning about being holy? Moreover, the passage challenges us to be fully resourced for our ministry of teaching God's Word.

The Old Testament reminds us that from the beginning God's creative Word or *dabar* powerfully shapes the landscape of the planet and redefines the cosmos. Genesis' opening hymn to creation tells us that when God speaks his word, things happen: 'And God said . . . And it was so . . . And God saw that it was good'. God's Word is ever active and formative in our lives today. Isaiah expresses the power of God's Word:

> For as the rain and snow come down from heaven,
>   and do not return there until they have watered the earth,
> making it bring forth and sprout,
>   giving seed to the sower and bread to the eater,
> so shall my word be that goes out from my mouth;
>   it shall not return to me empty,
> but it shall accomplish that which I purpose. (Isa. 55.10–11)

In the New Testament, John gives us new glimpses into the Creator Word made flesh. In speaking of the *logos* he echoes the Greek idea of Wisdom, *sophia* and the Hebrew *hokmot*, by which God shaped creation (cf. Prov. 8.22–31). The Word reveals the divine in signs and words. With Peter we say: 'Lord, to whom can we go? You have the words of eternal life' (John 6.68). The continual challenge for us as ministers to read Scripture in such a way that a dialectic conversation is brought about between the text and context: a creative interaction, an interplay. The text points first to the original context – the historical setting and the geography of the Holy Land; in the case of the Gospels, to the first-century world with its political and religious pressures. But it also speaks to today's context: to our present situation, often ugly, often messy . . . full of contradictions, paradoxes, injustices and questions. Of every passage, the minister must ask: 'how is this conversation going?'

The six major different types of Scripture shape the practice of ministry in different ways. The *historical books* challenge us to discern the action of God in history and in the present. As interpretations of events within a narrative-theology that seeks to make sense of the experience and vicissitudes of God's people, they invite us to identify and name the work of God in today's world. What is going on, and what is God up to today? The *prophetic books* present a special challenge to ministry today. They invite us to uncover hypocrisy and idolatry, and to recall God's people to courageously struggle for peace and justice and the true knowledge of God. *The Psalms* and poetic works have a cherished place in ministry today, as we identify with the hopes and hurts of the psalmist. They teach us not to hesitate in bringing to God in prayer our questions and our doubts. The *Wisdom literature* invites us to make sense of today's confusions by pondering anew the meaning of a life well lived, with the providence of God. In the *Gospels*, as I see how the evangelists found ideas to communicate the mystery of Christ, I am challenged to discover a Christology for today, faithful to the given tradition but alert and responsive to the pains and joys of the present movement. The *Letters* too invite us to do what Paul and the other writers did: to struggle to articulate the reality of salvation in language and concepts which resonate with today's world. If, for example, the language of 'justification by faith' makes sense primarily within the thought-world of the first century, the question becomes: what concepts, ideas and images must *we* use to communicate the wonder of life in Christ to our contemporary hearers?

Two approaches to reading Scripture are especially appropriate to the practice of ministry today. The discipline of *lectio divina*, the slow, ponderous, meditative reading of Scripture developed by Benedict and the monastic tradition, contrasts with today's frenetic, superficial speed reading. With its four stages, it has been likened to 'feasting on the Word'. First, *lectio* invites us to take a bite, to read a passage attentively, alert to particular words that strike us. Second, in *meditatio*, we can hold the word in our mind and heart as a piece of fruit might be held in the mouth: we take time to ask the Holy Spirit to lead us to its deepest meaning. Third, in *oratio*, we savour its taste, bitter or sweet or surprising, and allow this to lead us into a kind of prayer that dares ask questions of God: What are you saying? How might I have to change? In this phase, we expose to God's Word our deepest needs and hopes. The Word will heal, disturb, invigorate. Finally in *contemplatio*, we digest the Word, welcome the Word within our very selves, integrate it, interiorize it, absorb it into our very being.[2]

A second approach, pioneered by Ignatius of Loyola in the sixteenth century, invites us to use our imaginations vividly as we engage with the text, especially when we read the episodes from the life of Christ in the Bible. Ignatius asks us to use our five senses. Use your eyes to look at the scene, visualize it, imagine it in your mind's eye, place yourself into the picture and become one of the characters. Reach out in your imagination and touch with your fingertips the characters, the soil, the water, the physical aspects. Even smell the scents of the scene and taste the air, the food, the atmosphere. But above all, Ignatius says, open your ears and listen to what the characters are saying to each other, what they are saying to you and what God is saying to you through all this. For those of us in active ministry, this approach to Scripture once again slows us down and demands time and attention. It leads to clearer discernment of God's will for us in the practice of ministry. That is the point: engagement with the Word leads us to echo St Ignatius's own prayer: 'Take, O Lord, and receive my entire liberty, my memory, my understanding and my whole will. All that I am and all that I possess You have given me: I surrender it all to You to be disposed of according to Your will. Give me only Your love and Your grace; with these I will be rich enough.'[3]

The challenge for the newly ordained and newly licensed is to dare to engage daily in the risky business of exposing the mind and soul to God's Word. This requires the vulnerability and utter openness to surprises, as revealed in Mary at the Annunciation: we must be prepared to be disturbed and reshaped by the Word. Indeed, through our disciplined times of daily Scripture reading we must dare to change (cf. 2 Tim. 4.16–17).

---

2 For a helpful introductory tool, see M. B. Pennington, 1998, *Lectio Divina: Renewing the Ancient Practice of Praying the Scriptures*, New York: Crossroad.

3 For a useful introduction to this pattern of praying, see T. M. Gallagher, 2008, *An Ignatian Introduction to Prayer: Scriptural Reflections According to the Spiritual Exercises*, New York: Crossroad.

Formed by worship

Liturgical formation celebrates the way that God shapes and redirects us through worship. Through the action of the Holy Spirit, we are formed as we worship. This is true of all worship but can be seen most clearly in the celebration of the Eucharist.

The Eucharist reveals the Church as it should be: a community of faith in which different gifts and ministries are exercised.[4] In the Sunday Eucharist, the priest does not have to do every task. Rather, on behalf of the bishop, the priest *presides* over an array of ministries, standing back, as it were, and letting other people step forward. The priest *does not* necessarily have to personally welcome each worshipper; read all the Scriptures; lead the intercessions; lead the music . . . other people fulfill these ministries. The priest *does* have to be a focus of unity; hold the celebration together . . . absolve, consecrate, represent the people to God in the act of Thanksgiving; represent, in some way, Christ to the people; feed, bless. The image of priest as eucharistic president gives us a model of ministry which recovers the distinctive priestly task as spiritual leader, and encourages the proper development of lay ministries: the priest, both in and out of church, oversees in love the many and varied lay ministries within the Christian community.[5] In other words, the Eucharist itself can clarify the vocation of the priest: this is part of what we mean by liturgical formation – the formative effect of the liturgy upon us.

The Eucharist can be a place of profound affirmation for the priest, as the priestly identity and role are summed up very clearly and vividly in the various actions: what the priest or deacon does in church is to be done also outside in the community and in the world. There are ten particular moments which are most symbolic and iconic of the priestly ministry, which remind us what we are about.

Proclamation of the gospel: the deacon or priest is not here giving another reading: they are proclaiming the Word of Life, and all stand to listen to the voice of the living Christ. This encapsulates the very mission of the ordained: to speak out boldly the message of salvation.

Confession and absolution: the priest is called to lead people both to penitence and to the experience of forgiveness, both in liturgy and in the practice of pastoral care.

Intercession: while the president need not lead the prayers of the faithful, in good practice he or she should introduce and conclude them. This

---

4 P. McPartlan, 1993, *The Eucharist Makes the Church*, Edinburgh: T&T Clark.

5 R. Greenwood, 1999, *Transforming Priesthood: A New Theology of Mission & Ministry*, London: SPCK.

represents very poignantly how intercession is a place where the priest calls God's people to listen both to God and to the needs of the world, that they may offer themselves for involvement in God's mission. It is the moment in the celebration where priest and people are reminded of their vocation to be in touch with the passionate and compassionate heart-beat of God and with the pulse of a world in need of healing.

Sign of peace: as the priest calls God's people to a sign of mutual acceptance and reconciliation, around the table Christ forms a people in radical equality, community and dignity. Here we are offered a powerful image of our vocation to be reconcilers and agents of God's healing in a broken, fragmenting world.

Offertory: as the priest at the Offertory takes to the holy table the people's bread, 'which earth has given and human hands have made', so he or she will be seeking to lead people to surrender their daily work and labour to God. As the priest accepts the wine, so throughout the week in parish ministry he or she will be helping people to bring their sorrows and joys to God: the chalice holds 'wine to gladden the human heart' (Ps. 104.15) but also represents the cup of suffering (Mark 14.36). Accepting these as potentially God-revealing gifts encourages the priest to live out daily in the world a Christian approach to creation, a sacramental view of the universe, seeing all creation as God-bearing.

Thanksgiving: as the priest invites God's people to 'lift up their hearts' so he or she will seek to live a eucharistic life, marked by daily praise and fulfil the injunction to 'pray without ceasing, give thanks in all circumstances' (1 Thess. 5.17–18).

Consecration: as the priest takes bread and wine into his or her hands and asks that by the power of the Holy Spirit these natural elements may become for us the Body and Blood of Christ, so we see a powerful image of God's call to us to surrender into his hands the raw material of our lives, that we may become Christ-bearers for our needy world. As a eucharistic prayer in *Common Worship* puts it: 'form us into the likeness of Christ'. We find ourselves caught up into the movement of Christ's self-offering to the Father, as we make *anamnesis* (remembrance) of the cross.

Fraction: in the very breaking of the bread, priests see before their eyes the clearest possible expression of the ministry: to be consecrated for God and to be broken and given for the people. As the Ordination rite in the Catholic tradition puts it, at the giving of the chalice: 'Realize what you are doing; imitate what you handle.'

Communion: as the priest discovers the presence of Christ, in some way, in fragments of broken bread and in poured-out wine, so he or she will seek to fulfil Matthew 25's injunction: 'I was sick and you visited me', finding Christ in broken, fragile bread-like lives. The Eucharist, celebrating 'God with us' and 'the Word made flesh' in the physicality and materiality of created elements, prompts us to go out into God's world and become ever more alert to God's presence in human lives: to rediscover the sacramentality of all of life. St John Chrysostom (Hom. 50.3–4) asks:

> Do you wish to honour the body of Christ? Do not ignore him when he is naked. Do not pay him homage in the temple clad in silk, only then to neglect him outside where he is cold and ill-clad. He who said: 'This is my body' is the same who said: 'You saw me hungry and you gave me no food', and 'whatever you did to the least of my brothers you did also to me . . .' What good is it if the Eucharistic table is overloaded with golden chalices when your brother is dying of hunger? Start by satisfying his hunger and then with what is left you may adorn the altar as well.

Further, as priests offer Holy Communion to God's people, they will see in this action a reminder of the call to go out into the world to respond to both physical and spiritual hungers: to feed the poor and the spiritually hungry of the parish.

Blessing: as the priest blesses the people and sends them forth into mission, so he or she is reminded of their vocation to bless people's lives and to help enable and resource the ministry of all God's people.

In these ways elements within the Eucharist can inspire and empower mission. Indeed the Eucharist becomes a manifesto for mission, calling us to clear priorities. At the very heart of the Eucharist is the celebration of the cross, passion and resurrection of the Lord. It is the paschal mystery, the mystery of Easter, the mystery of God's sharing and redeeming our human pain, that will help make sense of the daily practice of ministry – rather, it is the key, the heart of parish ministry. What is proclaimed in the Eucharist – in both Word and Sacrament – is nothing less than the very message we will live out in our daily mission. The Eucharist clarifies and strengthens the vocation of the priest. If one may, in some way, act *in persona Christi* at the Lord's table, this is only to remind us that we are to do the same on the street, in the parish, in the home . . . One curate was discovering this for herself. The challenge for new ministers and training incumbents is that in order to experience the formational character of the Eucharist, we need to be more alert and aware at each celebration of the working of the Holy Spirit. As Irvine puts it: 'to elucidate the formational meaning of worship we need to work with a more developed pneumatology . . . and accordingly give a greater logical priority to the presence and active working of

God'.[6] The Eucharist is not just 'another service to be taken' – rather in it, as in all worship, God invites us to formation and transformation by the Holy Spirit. The Eucharist powerfully reminds us, on each occasion, of our mission and vocation. As Augustine put it (Sermon 272):

> If you, therefore, are Christ's body and members, it is your own mystery that is placed on the Lord's table! It is your own mystery that you are receiving! You are saying *Amen* to what you are: your response is a personal signature, affirming your faith. When you hear *The Body of Christ* you reply *Amen*. Be a member of Christ's body, that your *Amen* may ring true!

Formed by woundedness

The Eucharist, as we have seen, speaks to priests about their need to be broken and given. Priestly formation is deeply incised by the marks of vulnerability and woundedness. As Paul puts it: 'I have been crucified with Christ; and it is no longer I who live, but it is Christ who lives in me' (Gal. 2.19–20). Other images shine light on the costliness and personal pain involved in formation: the breaking and remoulding of the potter's vessel (Jer. 18), the pruning of the vine for greater fruitfulness (John 15).

Ministerial formation involves many dimensions of unmaking and re-making. For the newly ordained, the transition into a public role entails to some extent the loss of the private and 'mine': the curate learns that they now 'belong to the institution' – others have a claim on their time and gifts and sometimes this can be draining and inconvenient, especially where marital and family responsibilities are also carried. Some find as bereaving the transition from the supportive, intimate, safe community of peers in theological college or course to the parish situation where one is plunged into a cacophony of competing demands. And there can be an intensification of struggling with one's shadow side as now, as ordained, one is expected at all times to be a paragon of virtue. The challenge, for training ministers and curates alike, is to reclaim spaces for mutual affirmation, as well as for critique.

As Rolheiser reminds us, all Christian formation is essentially paschal in character.[7] He contrasts two types of death: a terminal death that ends

---

6 C. Irvine, 2005, *The Art of God: The Making of Christians and the Meaning of Worship*, London: SPCK, p. 85.

7 R. Rolheiser, 1988, *Seeking Spirituality: Guidelines for a Christian Spirituality for the Twenty-First Century*, London: Hodder and Stoughton, p. 187.

possibilities and a paschal death that opens one up to a new future. This casts light on the experience of priestly formation. A dying is taking place on different levels, a letting go. This is experienced at the time as something disorientating and painful. But the significant change taking place within the transition towards public ordained ministry is opening the person to many new possibilities. The paschal-like transition is not, however, limited to the passage towards ordination. Rather, it sets the pattern, even paradigm, for priestly growth throughout ministry. As Perri puts it: 'Mystical death is required . . . Priests need to contemplate the inner contradictions. By holding this chaos, the grace of God's aggressive and creative hand will refashion the indelible mark.'[8]

The place where we can work through a sense of woundedness and yield to God's healing and empowering grace may turn out to be the place of reflective prayer.

Formed by wonder

In our context, to wonder is recovering a sense of awe at what God is doing in our lives, to stand back and discern the movements of the Spirit. We are called to wonder: to think curiously and exploratively . . .

Recent research has revealed that ministerial formation advances most decisively by the discipline of regular and sustained theological reflection, in which reflective prayer forms a vital role.[9] The newly ordained and newly licensed ministers need to bring into the practice of active ministry the disciplines of theological reflection which were taught in theological college or course, and the training ministers need to ensure that their charges open up a reflective space where theological reflection can take place in the context of prayerful musings, in which prayer itself becomes a form of perception and deep knowing.

The practice of reflective prayer can be precisely the place where we learn to interpret the world, gain fresh perspective and insight and rekindle our vision of ministry. It can become inseparable and even indistinguishable from theological reflection: the place where we gain intuitions, glimpses into reality. Sometimes it helps to make the distinction between *head knowledge* and *heart knowledge*. The former conveys the need to gain intellectual and academic understanding of a subject, using our best

---

8 W. D. Perri, 1996, *A Radical Challenge for Priesthood Today*, Mystic, CT: Twenty-Third Publications, p. 98.

9 A. D. Mayes, 2009, *Spirituality in Ministerial Formation: The Dynamic of Prayer in Learning*, Cardiff: University of Wales Press.

powers of reasoning and analysis, while the latter speaks of a deeper way of knowing. The Eastern Churches commend the practice of *moving* or relocating the mind to the heart. As Simeon the New Theologian puts it:

> The mind should be in the heart . . . Keep your mind there (in the heart), trying by every possible means to find the place where the heart is, in order that, having found it, your mind should constantly abide there. Wrestling thus, your mind will find the place of the heart.[10]

Prayer becomes the place where we learn the deepest lessons about ministry and discern more clearly the action of God in our lives. We are invited again to consider the relationship of spirituality and theology: is theology a subject to be studied safely and dispassionately in the study or college, or does it rather spring from the life of prayer in which we struggle with God? In the first millennium, there was no separation of theology and spirituality. But in the West, the rise of scholasticism and the universities led to considering spirituality and theology as analytically distinct disciplines: scholarship was separated from *ascesis*. The study of theology became gradually divorced from the practice of spirituality, and the Enlightenment, seeing scientific enquiry as the way to truth, only served to reinforce this divide.

As we noted above, the Christian East did not follow this path. As Lossky put it:

> We must live the dogma expressing a revealed truth, which appears to us as an unfathomable mystery, in such a fashion that instead of as-similating the mystery to our mode of understanding, we should, on the contrary, look for a profound change, an inner transformation of spirit, enabling us to experience it mystically. Far from being mutually opposed, theology and mysticism support and complete each other. One is impossible without the other.[11]

Evagrius of Pontus (346–99) puts it very succinctly: 'The one who prays is a theologian; a theologian is one who prays.'[12]

Skills in theological reflection learnt in training must be carried forward and developed in the practice of parish ministry. Reflective exercises

---

10 Simeon the New Theologian, 'Three Methods of attention and prayer', in E. Kadloubovsky and G. E. H. Palmer, 1977, *Writings from the Philokalia*, London: Faber and Faber, p. 158.

11 V. Lossky, 1957, *The Mystical Theology of the Eastern Church*, Cambridge: James Clarke, p. 8.

12 A. Louth, 2000, *Theology and Spirituality*, Oxford: SLG Press, p. 4.

will help.[13] The training minister will want to model different patterns of theological reflection as absolutely essential to the practice of priesthood today.[14]

Reflective prayer, the kind of prayer that allows for meditation, contemplation and theological reflection, can thus become one of the key places where we do our deepest theology, where we make sense of ministry and discern what God is doing in our lives. The challenge to training ministers and curates is to be disciplined and consistent in opening up prayerful and reflective spaces amidst the routines and stresses of ministry. Particular effort might be given to the daily offices, especially to the practice of training minister and curate saying Evening Prayer together, followed by a space in which to process the events of the day. This was traditional, but is often squeezed out of current practice by the tyranny of competing demands on time. But here formation by Word, worship, woundedness and wonder comes together very powerfully. We turn to God at the end of a weary day and allow his Word to remould us and restore us. A space for unburdening to God the stresses and anxieties of the day enables a deep experience of God healing and balming our woundedness. In the reflective space we can offer to God the questions and dilemmas of the day and discern where God has been sensed, clarifying what God is saying to us. In his poem 'Evensong' the seventeenth-century priest-poet George Herbert collapses into his stall in church at the end of a day.[15] He asks God: 'What have I brought thee home for this thy love?' He finds Evening Prayer as a place where he can bring to God the trials, joys, questions and paradoxes of ministry. He comes before God in his fragility and vulnerability, and in his brokenness, and he surrenders to God the woes and heartaches of ministry to be touched and transfigured. Thus all the struggles of ministry flow into prayer, which becomes a place of inner transformation by the Holy Spirit. Herbert experienced prayer as the place of utter transparency before God. In prayer there is no place for false pleasantries, no place for masks, no pretending. In prayer we come before God just as we are, exposing to God our heartaches: the struggle for holiness; our sense of failure at times, our sense of unworthiness in celebrating the sacraments and in preaching; a sense of frustration, in not being effective, or not having accomplished what we wanted; a sense of guilt regarding those things 'left

---

13 See for example those recommended by J. Thompson, 2008, *SCM Study Guide to Theological Reflection*, London: SCM Press.

14 Good practice is exemplified in M. Paterson and J. Leach, 2008, *Pastoral Supervision: A Handbook*, London: SCM Press and K. Lamdin and D. Tilley, 2007, *Supporting New Ministries in the Local Church*, London: SPCK.

15 G. Herbert, 1995, *The Complete English Works*, London: Everyman's Library.

undone', people unvisited; we can surrender to God our financial, health or family worries. As Hebert puts it, such things are 'balls of wild-fire to my troubled mind'. But we can also discover this place of prayer to be not only healing but astonishingly creative. For dawning on Herbert is a new sense of perspective and a fresh awareness: 'My God, thou art all love . . . And in this love, more than in bed, I rest.'

In such times of prayer, then, we can regain a sense of wonder and practise the art of wondering: it is here that we may glimpse, most clearly, what God is doing in the work of formation.

PART 2

Development

4

The Teacher–Learner Relationship

SUE CROSS

Introduction

There is really too much to say about the significance of interpersonal relationships in professional development, and especially the teacher–learner relationship, for a short chapter. So, my goal is to present some selected thoughts on both theory and practice which can be contextualized within initial ministerial education. These thoughts should challenge some orthodox assumptions but support other, well-founded, practices. What they won't do is provide a simple 'road-map' to success: it doesn't exist. Better teaching supports better learning. It ultimately comes from the degree to which the teacher finds the developmental relationships in which they take part to be a source of deeper satisfaction, greater challenge and, by no means least, more fun. As one side of a creative dialogue, this chapter may help to encourage and sustain the reflective process which accompanies professional practice. Above all, I hope to inspire those entrusted with the development of future generations and encourage those who aspire to mature ministry themselves.

Experiential learning

The transition from student to novice professional is always going to be a significant one. Ordination as a deacon at the start of a parish ministry may also add a unique dimension. In any event, if learning is to continue after college for any novice professional, it must be characterized by a different approach to who the 'teacher' now is, and what 'teaching' might look like. Some of the relationships already built and sustained with tutors may provide clues about what to expect but it will not be the same. And, indeed, the ideas and preconceptions of the person(s) tasked with helping and guiding that novice professional may also be challenged. Thus, while 'experiential learning' may have informed and contributed to the pedagogy of college teaching, in the parish it becomes essential.

Experiential learning is probably a term you already know – it is becoming a rather 'old wine' – but, through the years, its meaning has become thin and insipid. It has been diluted too frequently, losing much of the flavour it once had. We need to rediscover the potency of the wine itself, enjoy what it can do for us, and celebrate in the proper fashion. Unlike the parable, it will not take a miracle for us to enjoy the best wine even rather late in the party. All that is necessary is to think more precisely about what experiential learning actually means.

One of the key twentieth-century educationists, John Dewey, talked about the 'threshold concept'[1] of experiential learning in a lecture given in 1938 (although the version referenced here was not published until 1997). He outlined the conditions which govern learning from experience as a call to modernize the education of children. Dewey (and theorists such as Kolb who applied his thinking to adult learning) focuses attention on the way that what we do and what we *think* about what we do (as well as what we have done, and might do next) can be a fundamental source for effective learning. It can complement learning from systematic study of relevant texts and is most likely to be important where propositional knowledge is to be combined with the practical wisdom of professional work. Experiential learning is what we all need if we are to convert what happens to us into an ability to refine, enhance and improve our own performance.

Dewey identified three important elements which ensure that experience leads to *learning* not just the repetition of activity. First, he said that continuity of experience mattered and that

> the principle of continuity of experience means that every experience both takes up something from those which have gone before and modifies in some way the quality of those which come after.[2]

In other words, what we did in the past affects what we are doing in the present and will do in the future. However, experiencing the world in a more or less random way will not maximize the learning potential of an environment for beneficial growth. Experiential learners need to become selective about experiences through which to learn and how to relate to such experience. This is a task for which their 'teacher' (whoever that may be) may be well qualified to assist – although 'assistance' of course does

---

1 J. H. F. Meyer and R. Land, 2003, 'Threshold concepts and Troublesome Knowledge: Linkages to ways of thinking and Practising within the Disciplines', Occasional Report 4. ETL Project. Universities of Edinburgh, Coventry and Durham. Accessed on line on 18th June 2011 at www.etl.tla/docs/ETLreport4/pdf.

2 J. Dewey, 1997, *Experience and Education*, New York: Touchstone, p. 35.

not mean 'do on their behalf', which would itself deprive the learner of one of the experiences from which they might learn.

If an understanding of *'continuity'* is essential to experiential learning so also are *'situation'* and *'interaction'*. These were the second and third elements identified by Dewey. 'Situation' means that learning is located in a specific context or environment. 'Interaction' requires learners to participate and engage actively with the material or substance of their experience for its potential to be unlocked. But what is the significance of these terms? Traditional pedagogy takes place in a highly specific and precisely defined location (the formal classroom) and includes a constrained and directed form of interaction (such as systematic absorption of texts and the answering of questions chosen by other people). Dewey did not set out to deny that, under certain circumstances and for some material, this is the most effective way to acquire information. Yet his discussion of situation and interaction also provided the basis to argue in favour of a much richer appreciation of the potential for learning outside the classroom and within the context of more democratic relationships between learner and teacher. Writing of interaction, he said:

> An experience is always what it is because of a transaction taking place between an individual and what, at the time, constitutes his environment, whether the latter consists of persons with whom he is talking about some topic or event, the subject talked about . . . the toys with which he is playing . . . the book he is reading . . . or the materials of an experiment he is performing. The environment, in other words, is whatever conditions interact with personal needs, desires, purposes and capacities to create the experience which is had . . . Continuity and interaction in their active union with each other provide the measure of the educative significance and value of an experience.[3]

Experiential learning requires the learner and the teacher to work together to appreciate, manage and exploit the learning potential of the environment. The development or use of a 'learning environment' is one of the core professional skills of a teacher.[4] However, when we focus upon the social aspects of the learning environment in the twenty-first-century Church, as we do here, the 'learning environment' is to a large extent the relationship between the teacher and the learner. So, who are the teachers?

---

3 Dewey, *Experience*, pp. 43–5.
4 Sue Cross, 2009, *Adult Teaching and Learning*, Maidenhead: Open University Press, pp. 33–53.

First and foremost, when discussing 'teachers' and 'learners' in the context of this book, you may anticipate a discussion of the relationship between training incumbents and curates. This is of course necessary but, on its own, perhaps not sufficient. The incumbent comes closest to our formal notion of 'teacher' (which is inspired by schools and colleges) and certainly bears much of that privilege and responsibility – but there are also many other people who will contribute to learning. Indeed, this sharing of teaching responsibility is arguably vital if the novice professional is to grow into a ministry which will encompass a wide variety of professional, pastoral and vocational relationships. Specifically, a ministerial role may also be 'taught' by lay members of the parish (office holders and not), other professionals (musicians, teachers, police officer, administrators, caretakers, funeral directors, photographers/film makers, doctors, social workers, charitable aid workers etc.), other Christian clergy and representatives of other faith communities. The significant and unique responsibility with which the incumbent will be entrusted is to ensure that the learning potential of the parish into which the curate is licensed (or where other recognized ministries are being developed) is fully realized so that it effectively supports the vocational and professional aspects of ministerial development. This may also entail helping the 'learner' to make sense of – and appreciate – what they can learn from the broad faculty of 'teachers' in their parish.

If we accept the notion that, in this context, the learning environment is primarily the web of learning relationships, we should also ask how an incumbent can help with the management of the learning experiences. Broadly, the challenge will be to appreciate which previous influences may be in play, as well as helping to manage the elements of current experience to maximize their capacity for growth (while also managing risk to other people involved in such processes) and ensuring that the positive learning outcomes are consolidated into future performance. More simply, the success of the teaching relationship requires a *shared* appreciation of what is actually going on. It will have an affective component but it should be deliberately and thoughtfully managed by both sides. It is likely to benefit from reflection separately and together.

In discussing the role that the experienced minister can play in helping someone more recently entrusted with a ministerial function, we must sound a note of caution. Most adults seem to thrive in learning environments which sustain quite high levels of personal autonomy. Therefore, a balance needs to be found between maximizing an adult learner's potential (delivering the content) while respecting and nurturing the independence and autonomy which is necessary for the learner as an adult and as a novice. The importance of this balance is even more acute as this training environment also has to be a fully functioning parish: the incumbent needs to ensure that the learning supports progress towards greater autonomy in learning and in execution of the duties entrusted to the learner. Again, the key point is the relationship: the necessary balance will be most easily struck when there is a relationship which enables guidance into situations which offer the appropriate level of experience consolidated by appropriate reflection upon action. This is no easy task. Back to Dewey, who clearly described the educator's responsibility in this context:

> They should know how to utilize the surroundings, physical and social, that exist so as to extract from them all that they have to contribute to building up experiences that are worthwhile.[5]

Dewey had previously described the attributes of this kind of teacher:

> it is his business to be on the alert . . . to judge what attitudes are actually conducive to continued growth and what are detrimental. He must in addition have that sympathetic understanding of individuals as individuals which gives him an idea of what is actually going on in the minds of those who are learning.[6]

We should make no mistake: the stakes are high. For example, I have been told that most fruitful ordained ministries are based upon a successful curacy. The quality of the experience continues to shape and inform the life of the priest for many years. Learning to recognize the influences of the past on present activity, to analyse the particular effects of the current situation and to choose action to enhance interaction with the best elements from which to learn is at the core of the experiential learning process which underpins such successful curacies. Experiential learning in professional practice was in the past largely assumed to be effective, of high quality and safe in the hands of well-meaning and more experienced colleagues. For many people it did in fact work well and was a source of more or less unconscious growth and improvement. However, for at least some others, this powerful learning experience was damaging. Some never recovered from it as their sense of vocation was undermined. At best, such individuals were less effective than they might have been. At worst, they gave up in failure and disappointment. Nobody has been indifferent to

---

5 Dewey, *Experience*, p. 39.
6 Dewey, *Experience*, p. 40.

this issue but it has not been given the explicit attention in all cases that it undoubtedly deserves.

So, now let's consider how to achieve some of these challenging ideals.

How do relationships influence learning?

Much educational theory has been rooted in psychological analysis of the way individuals acquire information and new behaviour. However, in the context of this chapter, we have already seen that learning is not confined to the mind of the learner, or even the minds of one teacher and one learner. As Dewey and later theorists recognized, learning is environmentally situated and socially determined: in other words, we learn together. We should briefly consider how this happens.

Anyone developing their ministry joins a 'community of practice' situated within the wider Church. Lave and Wenger coined the term 'legitimate peripheral participation' to describe one of the ways new members of diverse cultures and organizations acquire relevant practical and propositional knowledge. They say that:

> Legitimate peripheral participation provides a way to speak about the relationship between newcomers and old-timers, and about activities, identities, artefacts and communities of knowledge and practice. It concerns the process by which newcomers become part of a community of practice.[7]

This informal and often apparently unstructured activity is widely found in vocational and professional settings and is a particular kind of experiential learning. Their work illuminates a process of discovering how to *be* something or someone rather than just doing a job. It is radically different from the objective-driven, tightly structured, individualistic approach found in some training regimes. In later work, Wenger continued to describe fully how communities of practice define themselves through a combination of participation in the pursuit of the shared aims and by the design and creation of the particular tools, processes, rules and materials which are required for the refined, purposeful engagement in the common endeavour.[8] This includes the manner in which status is acquired

---

7 J. Lave and E. Wenger, 1991, *Situated Learning: Legitimate Peripheral Participation*, Cambridge: Cambridge University Press, p. 29.

8 E. Wenger, 1998, *Communities of Practice: Learning, Meaning, and Identity*, Cambridge: Cambridge University Press.

(the progress from novice to expert) by learning to take part in essential activities while using the socially determined techniques, equipment and procedures which are specific to that community. The way in which relationships are conducted will have a significant influence on the successful transmission of techniques, values and standards (many of which may be locally variable, tacit and controversial) to new members of a community. Learning to work within a community requires a balance of activity working alongside others (who are themselves at different stages of development) as well as undertaking tasks alone. To put it in the language of the Church, a vocation is not just something one does but one lives. And living is done in community with others.

The most important implication of this perspective is that adult learners, including ministers, must not be too busy 'doing stuff'. They need time to associate with other people in order to listen, watch and reflect (critically and theologically) on what they are experiencing. This should be easier for clergy to appreciate than it is for some other professionals. Yet, sometimes, it seems hard to achieve. Newcomers may feel that after years of training before ordination or appointment to a new recognized role in ministry they are there to work *for* the parish. They need to experience some good examples of working *with* it.

Moreover, individuals and groups may enable a challenging situation to become achievable in the early years of practice by enabling the learner to achieve things which cannot be managed alone. This kind of 'scaffolding' provides a sense of achievement.[9] It motivates the learner to continue to struggle with the process of learning because they can experience what it will feel like to be able to succeed (eventually) at something which is currently beyond them. The sense of shared achievement strengthens the trust between novices and more experienced partners in the process. It is also a cumulative experience which can gradually enable roles to be rotated, enabling experienced partners also to learn new approaches to familiar activities. Learning by adults is, very genuinely, a team effort.

Finally, we should consider the notion of transformative learning. Adults who have recently qualified to develop a new role undertake the early years of their practice with an enormous amount of accumulated experience which will influence their work. As we have already noted, this will in turn be transformed by their first experiences of a life which has been entrusted with new responsibilities. It is the work of any experienced colleague entrusted with the development of new members of their

---

9 K. Tusting and D. Barton, 2006, *Models of Adult Learning: A Literature Review*, Leicester: NIACE. For an introduction to the work of Bruner and Vygotsky in this area, see pp. 13–14.

community to appreciate the novice's past, evaluate her/his needs, design specific opportunities, evaluate and reflect upon outcomes and feed such knowledge into further design before finally assessing performance in key tasks. This is a considerable responsibility and one which some might find daunting. It is likely that both partners in a learning relationship will be changed by it.

Mezirow observed that deep-seated change in an individual's guiding frames of reference is very hard to achieve, but such 'perspective trans-formation' may be most likely to happen when people are confronted by 'disorienting dilemmas'. The relationship between transformative learning theory and formation and theological education is fully explored by Sorensen – but here it is sufficient to underline the particular responsibility that anyone promoting adult learning must consider.[10] I shall spell it out. Learners need to be equipped to deal with the effects of the learning being promoted – which means that the teacher, probably an incumbent, has a duty of care for the learner as well as for the people whom she/he will encounter in the performance of duties. Some aspects of parish life may confront anyone with ministerial responsibilities with dilemmas which are indeed highly disorienting. There must be opportunity to process such encounters in a supportive and safe way. Although this sounds straight-forward it may not always be so. The relationships, including those between priests and deacons, Readers or pastoral assistants will be multi-faceted. It may not always seem appropriate to discuss a situation honestly with the person who will in due course assess your competence. It is vital that, through post-ordination and other training arrangements or men-toring and other informal relationships, there is always a non-hierarchical relationship in which to explore sensitive issues in a safe, honest and supportive way. The training incumbent or other entrusted with respon-sibility for ministerial development may from time to time also need such support.

What is so distinctive about ordained ministry?

Having looked through some more general 'lenses' at the issues in this chapter, we should now spare a thought for the specific context in which priests live, work, teach and learn. These will be specific to the develop-ment of ordained ministers but they will impact directly and indirectly on everyone else in a parish one way or another.

---

10 Christine A. Sorensen, 2007, *Formation, Transformation, Transformative Learning, and Theological Education*, unpublished PhD thesis. University of Auckland.

Although this may now be changing, attitudes to the formation of novice professionals (ministerial development) in the Church of England have historically seemed to lag behind those influencing other professions such as medicine, education, social work and the law. The role of training incumbent may come to illuminate other aspects of clergy life, but such beneficial outcomes are by no means inevitable. Some incumbents have simply viewed the arrival of a curate as 'another pair of hands' to share the work of busy parish life. This needs rethinking under the new terms and conditions of service and new arrangements for initial ministerial education (IME). Most professions require their new members to undertake a period of supervised practice after they have passed an entry grade qualification. We have already looked at a small sample of the research (see also the references at the end of the chapter). Such understandings are, in my view, all relevant to the training practices of Church of England ministry. However, there is more about this particular situation which I now want to consider.

This learning relationship is different from those in other professions for the following reasons:

1. The call to ordained ministry in the Church of England may be seen as significantly different from many other occupations.
2. Curates and their training incumbents are resident in the same parish for three years or more.
3. Professional training is linked to vocational formation into a priestly ministry (which is not an uncontested concept).
4. Progression is limited to a single 'employer' (the Church of England). Changes to the terms and conditions of service mean new clergy will be entering a church which is significantly different from the one in which their teachers began ministry.
5. Issues of gender and professional/vocational development are even more complex and sensitive than they are in most other occupations.

We should consider at least briefly some of the implications for the learning relationship of each of these factors.

First, the vocational context. It may be tempting to consider the priestly vocation a mysterious and unique encounter between God and an individual, the practical outworkings of which are not necessarily amenable to human reasoning. Those who believe this to be the case may have some difficulty considering a cognitively based approach to a learning relationship. For them, it may be that a call to ordained ministry requires only prayer, biblical study and working out in practice the details of that ministry to which the individual is directed by God through the Holy Spirit. I do not wish to undermine such an approach. I cannot, however, fully endorse it, if it is limited only to ordained ministry and is used as a reason to be unreflective about ways of developing both the talents and vocation to which one is called. I do believe that Christians in any profession or occupation have a particular duty to enable their own vocation to live up to the life to which they have been called and to assist and support others in developing vocationally. This is an obligation to do what is required by a particular calling in a way which is constantly informed by a desire to practise the presence of God – and thoughtful appreciation of the insights of sound learning practice may tend to enable, rather than disable, this process. When we are sustaining one another in following the path to which we believe God has called them and us, we both exercise a greater responsibility but are given far greater resources from which to draw.

Second, let's look at the residential context. Living 'over the shop' can provide rich opportunities for learning – but there can also be difficulty ensuring adequate time for rest and relaxation away from work. Learning in the parish is greatly enriched by living a shared Christian life but such ideas are prone to becoming 'idealized'. At best, it is an enormous opportunity to deepen and bless the growth of vocation and enhance professional competence through immersion in the learning environment. However, as in all powerful learning environments, it can also be a source of oppression and exploitation. The introduction of learning contracts into the process of curacy is easily lampooned by those who are resistant to change. Yet at their best they can be an effective tool to enable both sides of a relationship to establish a clear and reasonable understanding of what each side may expect of the other: they help to sketch some boundaries in a shared space. The relationship between a curate and their incumbent is not a friendship (although, at best, it should be friendly in character). It is one in which power is unequally distributed and where both sides may have expectations which can easily become misaligned. In negotiating the learning contract and reviewing it systematically, at least annually, both parties can raise concerns in a timely and non-threatening way and seek to establish corrective action. Without such a process difficult situations tend to fester and it is not unknown for the relationship to break down. Let's remember Lave and Wenger's research and the idea of legitimate peripheral participation (or the value of hanging out with the 'old timers'). A parish is graced by abundant opportunity for learning to be based upon the Holy Spirit's work expressed through serious encounters with the rich eccentricity of human lives. We plan meticulously and engage thoroughly so that there is space to be surprised by the joy of learning for its own sake, as well as training to improve competence.[11]

Third, I will touch lightly again on the development of the priestly vocation entwined with professional roles. I am grateful to Irena Edgcumbe for her scholarly insight into the training of curates (the subject of her MA dissertation at UCL). As her supervisor, I learned a lot about the way a parish priest with a wider responsibility for some aspects of IME deepened her own understanding of the history of ministerial formation and current changes in Church of England practice. That supervisory relationship was a model for my discussions here. It was built upon mutual respect, common purpose and faithful commitment to a deepening spiritual growth alongside the discipline of academic study. Irena's study introduced me to alternative models of development for Christian ministry. *Paideia* comes from the Greek and suggests a process of formation through prayerful interaction with wise guides, while *Wissenschaft*, a German term, implies greater similarity with a professional training and development process leading towards overall technical competence. Whichever of these contrasting approaches is dominant in local practice, the relationships which surround the curate in training may enhance or inhibit spiritual growth as well as providing opportunities for the modelling of technical competence in the performance of fundamental tasks. The wise guide provides space for mistakes to be made without dire consequences, space for reflection when the learner is not too exhausted by activity, and kind encouragement along difficult paths. Such learning relationships sustain the formation of reflective and proficient ministers.

Fourth, those preparing others for ministry are doing so in a period of considerable change. The biggest challenge for teachers is to prepare learners for a future which they have not already experienced for themselves. Priests are not alone in doing this, but it is a more recent problem for them. Dewey's thoughts are particularly relevant here. If the teacher truly respects the significance of continuity of experience, situatedness and interaction then there is trust in the process of experiential learning: it will enable the learner to continue to learn whatever conditions prevail in the future. The corollary is true: trying to shape a novice into a pre-formed pattern, governed by yesterday's conditions, is likely neither to equip the novice for the uncertain future nor to provide them with a means by which they can successfully adapt when that future arrives.

Last, we should touch on matters of gender. It follows as a specific instance of the changes mentioned generically above. What impact might an

---

11 See also Cross, *Adult Teaching*, p. 151 and M. Csikszentmihalyi, 1990, *Flow*, New York: HarperCollins.

inclusive ordained ministry have on the Church of England? At best, we can expect a more fully human, empathic and creatively engaged clergy. At worst, we might fear schism. This chapter is too short for me to address feminist pedagogy in any depth, and so I simply direct interested readers to works by Belenky et al. and Gilligan to read alongside the feminist theology with which many will already be familiar.[12] The titles of these books alone – *Women's Ways of Knowing* and *In a Different Voice* – prompt a thought. Gender, psychological type, social class, sexual orientation and ethnicity all create differences in the way adults take in information about the world and process it. An excellent learning relationship recognizes such differences and encourages learning of how we can become our best selves through action and reflection upon our practice. Where there is no natural warmth or affection, no friendly character to relations, this is a tall order. Yet, on the other hand, if we take Jesus as our model teacher, we can ask nothing else of ourselves or of each other.

How do we know how well we are doing?

The House of Bishops engaged in extensive work on developing learning outcomes for ministerial education which, when published, provoked mixed reactions. We can respond with a tired yawn of jaded experience of other systems designed to accredit vocational competence which become expensive and bureaucratic or we can get angry about the loss of trust in the ability of experienced priests to train their successors in ways which have served the Church well for centuries. Or, we can welcome them for what they are: a tool – albeit imperfect – designed to help us do a difficult job better. All professions and professionals evaluate themselves and their performance: controversy tends to come only about the yardstick used to do the job.

A tool like the learning outcomes can assist learners and teachers to review and reflect creatively and prayerfully on progress and growth within an agreed framework. It may enhance our understanding of the situation within which the development is taking place and enable a sharing of wisdom from many years of faithful service. Any systematic approach can be dismissed as 'ticking boxes' and so it should be – if it is implemented crudely, without care and time, or as a substitute for sustained rigorous engagement. However, those licensed to ordained ministry are inducted into a national church with responsibility for complex legal, practical and highly sensitive activities and situations. The Church has a duty of care to

12 M. F. Belenky et al., 1986, *Women's Ways of Knowing*, New York: Basic Books and C. Gilligan, 1982, *In a Different Voice*, Cambridge, MA: Harvard University Press.

ensure that clergy are enabled to carry out such demanding responsibilities in a healthy, consistent and effective way. It would be irresponsible not to invest the very best thought and prayerful reflective practices in assisting those entrusted with individual training through nationally sustained standards in which to share. The standards represented by the learning outcomes should not be considered as fixed or inflexible. As they are used in learning practice by thoughtful ministers they can be further refined and made more precisely fit for use. However, this process is dependent on the national church taking ownership of this process and reflecting collectively upon the contribution it can make. Ideally, it might shed some light not just on development for curates but also upon the understanding of clerical practice at all stages of ordained ministry and the ways that ordained clergy interact with everyone else.

It should also be considered that the adoption of nationally agreed learning outcomes need not be the only basis for review of progress in the learning relationship between training incumbent and curate. Once a dialogue is established, and time is routinely made for the necessary dialogue, then those involved in the relationship should feel free to identify particular areas of development which can be marked and where success can be celebrated. Indeed, this is partly envisaged by the learning outcomes which include reference to personality and character, helping to define the necessary quality of the relationship between learner and teacher. The detail of such relationships will – and should – vary enormously, but they should all stand up to scrutiny. Both 'teacher' and 'learner' have much to gain from benchmarking themselves and each other against some agreed standards. Their relationship should be one of mutual encouragement, each recognizing the contribution made by the other to the success of the learning relationship. During a long (and sometimes exhausting) ministry the habit of review, refreshment and refocus effectively begun in the early years of ministry can be usefully sustained. This provides a basis for clergy review and a healthier anticipation of engagement in the whole Church. Loneliness and isolation can on occasions be a characteristic of parish ministry. Perhaps these are steps towards tackling such personally debilitating and collectively distressing problems.

A final word about fun

At the start of this chapter I said that '"Better" teaching, ultimately, comes from the degree to which the teacher finds the developmental relationships in which they take part to be a source of deeper satisfaction, greater challenge and, by no means least, more fun.' I haven't actually said much about 'fun' yet – but in defining the kinds of relationships upon which teaching and learning in a parish depend I have been trying to describe a model of relationships which are simply that. All activities and relationships which enable and facilitate learning should be 'fun'. Most adults thrive if the atmosphere and ethos of a learning encounter enables them to enjoy what they do, and to feel valued and safe as they struggle to improve. 'Fun' may be contrasted with 'fear' which generates emotions which tend to inhibit learning.[13]

Any ministry in the Church of England is a very serious business – but, if it is to reflect the light of Christ in a dark world, it also has to be a joyful one. I have no doubt that the source of that joy is the daily renewal of the deep personal relationship with Jesus. He called us to a life characterized by abundance and that includes the sustained joy in relating to the world created for us to share and to each other within it. Let us ensure that the relationship between learners and teachers never reflects anything less.

Further reading

J. S. Atherton, 2011, *Doceo; Competence, Proficiency and Beyond* [Online: UK] retrieved 28th March 2011 from http://www.doceo.co.uk/background/expertise.htm.

S. Brookfield, 1986, *Understanding and Facilitating Adult Learning*, Milton Keynes: Open University Press.

S. Brookfield, 1987, *Developing Critical Thinkers*, San Francisco: Jossey-Bass.

J. Dewey, 1991, *How We Think*, New York: Prometheus Books.

I. Edgcumbe, 2010, 'Work in progress: the implementation of national training guidelines for newly ordained clergy in the Church of England, unpublished MA dissertation. University College London.

Jennifer M. Gore, 1993, *The Struggle for Pedagogies*, London: Routledge.

J. Mezirow and Associates, 1990, *Fostering Critical Reflection in Adulthood*, San Francisco: Jossey-Bass.

J. Mezirow, 1991, *Transformative Dimensions of Adult Learning*, San Francisco: Jossey-Bass.

J. Mezirow, 2000, *Learning as Transformation*, San Francisco: Jossey-Bass.

---

13 Cross, *Adult Teaching*, pp. 111–29.

A. Rogers, 2002, *Teaching Adults*, 3rd edition, Maidenhead: Open University Press.

I. Salzberger-Wittenberg et al., 1983, *The Emotional Experience of Learning and Teaching*, London: Routledge and Kegan Paul.

D. Schön, 1991, *The Reflective Practitioner*, Aldershot: Ashgate.

5

Asking Questions

ROGER MATTHEWS

I keep six honest serving-men
(They taught me all I knew);
Their names are What and Why and When
And How and Where and Who.
(Rudyard Kipling, *The Elephant's Child*, 1902)

Some years ago, four people were interviewed for a new job. Somehow I was appointed even though it looked as if the others all had more experience. It was only later that I discovered I got the job not because of the brilliance of my answers in the interview but because I asked the best questions!

This is not to say that knowledge, qualifications or experience are unimportant – far from it! But to be an effective minister and leader, we also need to have the capacity to observe, reflect and continue to learn. And to do that, we need to be able to ask good questions – of ourselves, of others and of the organizational systems we encounter.

In his book, *Leading with Questions*, Michael Marquardt asserts that the best leaders are those who ask good questions and leading with questions improves organizations. 'Leaders who lead with questions will create a more humane workplace as well as a more successful business.'[1] However, he notes that the art of asking questions is often not encouraged as it can be seen as a sign of weak leadership rather than competence. Other reasons he mentions include a natural desire to protect ourselves from vulnerability, lack of time, lack of training or an organizational culture that expects leaders to provide answers or cannot cope with challenges to existing assumptions and policies. Changing this situation requires both the development of personal skills and altering the cultural expectations of the organization.

Marquardt's objective is to encourage leaders to create what he calls a *Questioning Culture* 'in which responsibility is shared. And when responsibility is shared, ideas are shared, problems are shared (problems are not yours or mine

---

1 M. J. Marquardt, 2005, *Leading with Questions*, San Francisco, CA: Jossey-Bass, p. 6.

but *ours*), and ownership of results is shared'.[2] He says a questioning culture exists when the people in it

- are willing to admit, 'I don't know'
- go beyond allowing questions; they encourage questions
- are helped to develop skills needed to ask questions in a positive way
- focus on asking empowering questions and avoid disempowering questions
- emphasize the process of asking questions and searching for answers rather than finding the 'right' answers
- accept and reward risk taking.[3]

I am not convinced that simply asking good questions will produce a great leader, but I am certainly persuaded that the ability to ask good questions is a mark of good leadership.

In this chapter, I invite you to come on a tour through history and across traditions and disciplines to reflect on the power of asking good questions. As we explore the landscape please bring your own history and context with you to see what new questions emerge that might be helpful to your own learning and practice of ministry.

The discipline of asking questions as a pathway to learning and transformation is not new. Socrates (died *c*.399 BC) is perhaps the earliest teacher and philosopher credited with promoting the deliberate and systematic use of questions. He taught his pupils to use questions to get under the surface of presenting issues or problems in an attempt to remove ambiguity or contradiction. This made him a natural challenger of the established norms and culture of his day. Eventually the political system of the time could no longer cope with him and he was sentenced to death by drinking poison. It is a sobering reflection that Socrates' fate is likely to be shared, albeit to a lesser extent, by all who challenge cultural norms with too many questions, or too much truth, too quickly. The path of questioning can be a dangerous one!

Biblical questions

God frequently uses questions to help his people understand their situation and notice their need to act or think differently. However, it is interesting to note that the first question in the Bible is asked by the serpent: 'Did God really say, "You must not eat from any tree in the garden?"'

---

2 Marquardt, *Leading with Questions*, p. 38.
3 Marquardt, *Leading with Questions*, p. 29.

(Gen. 3.1, NIV). This is quickly followed by God's first question to human-kind: 'Where are you?' (Gen. 3.9). These two questions offer a powerful contrast. In both cases the questioner already knew the answer to the question but their motivations for asking were very different. The serpent's question was manipulative and raised doubts about what God has said. In contrast, God's question is the beginning of a dialogue to help Adam and Eve understand their predicament. This raises an ethical dimension to the use of questions – not all questions are good questions.

Good questions, in both the quality and ethical senses, invite people to receive new information, or reconsider old assumptions, or accept a new call or commission. Trevor Hudson in the preface to his devotional book, *Questions God Asks Us*,[4] suggests that God's use of questions invites a conversation, affirms the dignity of human beings and makes the offer of transformation. He picks ten biblical questions for reflection by his readers, which are well worth pondering for ourselves: Where are you? (Gen. 3.9); Where is your brother? (Gen. 4.9); What is that in your hand? (Exod. 4.2); What is your name? (Gen. 32.27); What are you doing here? (1 Kings 19.13); What are you looking for? (John 1.38); Who do you say I am? (Matt. 16.15); Do you want to get well? (John 5.6); Why are you crying? (John 20.13,15); and Do you understand what I have done for you? (John 13.12).

Jesus was a master questioner. Hudson claims in his preface that of the 183 questions that Jesus is asked in the four Gospels, he only directly answers three! Perhaps this indicates that Jesus was less interested in offering answers than in enabling reflection and learning in each individual's context. It seems to me that his questions fall into seven general categories, all of which challenge, or even undermine, preconceived ideas.

- Jesus used questions as a teaching method, for example: 'Why are you thinking these things? Which is easier: to say to this paralysed man, "Your sins are forgiven", or to say, "Get up, take your mat and walk"?' (Mark 2.8–9, NIV). 'Now which of them will love him more?' (Luke 7.42). 'Do you see this woman?' (Luke 7.44). 'What is written in the law? How do you read it?' (Luke 10.26). 'Which of these three do you think was a neighbour to the man who fell into the hands of robbers?' (Luke 10.36).
- He used questions to enable events to be understood in a new way: for example, when Jesus was 'lost' in Jerusalem as a child, 'Why were

---

4 T. Hudson, 2008, *Questions God Asks Us*, Cape Town: Struik Christian Gifts. Also available in part at http://books.google.co.uk (accessed 21st May 2011).

you searching for me?' 'Didn't you know I had to be in my Father's house?' (Luke 2.49).

- His questions moved people towards a decision or commitment: for example at Caesarea Philippi he asks 'Who do people say the Son of Man is? . . . 'But what about you? . . . Who do you say I am?' (Matt. 16.13–15).

- He used questions to expose the most important issues not simply what is seen on the surface, for example, in stilling the storm: 'Where is your faith?' (Luke 8.25); and after the resurrection: 'Why do you seek the living among the dead?' (Luke 24.5).

- His questions opened and sustained encounters that brought learning to others: for example he asked the woman at the well 'Will you give me a drink?' (John 4.7).

- Jesus avoided assuming the obvious but checked whether individuals understood the consequences of what he was doing and gave them the responsibility to decide, for example: 'Do you want to get well?' (John 5.6). 'What do you want me to do for you?' (Mark 10.36).

- Finally, Jesus demonstrated that it is safe to ask the fundamental or unanswerable questions: 'My God, my God, why have you forsaken me?' (Matt. 27.46).

Most of these remain fruitful questions for personal and corporate reflection and, if we are to be faithful to the example of Jesus, it might be wise for us to move away from the type of study material that is based on fact and assertion and towards resources that invite an exploration of questions. This is inherently more risky and certainly a challenge for preachers and home-group leaders but is perhaps more consistent with biblical revelation. A helpful model is provided in Luke's Gospel in the post-resurrection narrative of the two disciples' journey to Emmaus where Jesus asks questions and listens before offering any response (Luke 24.13–35). This connects with the ministry of spiritual direction where the exploration of meaning and vocation are of primary concern and can be explored through the responses to two further biblical questions: 'Amazed and perplexed, they asked one another, "What does this mean?"' (Acts 2.12) and 'Whom shall I send. And who will go for us?' (Isa. 6.8).

Spiritual traditions

As well as the questions that God asks of human beings, there is a strong biblical record of the questions that we ask of God. This 'reverse' questioning is also a means of learning as we bring all our human capacity and frailty into God's presence. This is a common feature of the Psalms, for example in the repeated 'How long . . .?' questions in Psalm 13. It is also a feature of Jewish spirituality, for example, in Elie Wiesel's *Night*:

> Young Elie's spiritual master, Moche, tells him that every question possesses a power that does not lie in its answer. 'Man raises himself toward God by the questions he asks Him,' Moche explains. He adds that he cannot understand God's answers. When Wiesel asks him why, then, he prays, Moche replies: 'I pray to the God within me that He will give me the strength to ask Him the right questions.'[5]

Bethamie Horowitz, a social psychologist, expresses the different way that Jewish people approach learning and the use of questions in an article entitled *A Tradition of Questioning Tradition*. Here is one example:

> This habit of questioning and wrestling brings to mind a story about Nobel laureate Isidor Rabi, who attributed his becoming a scientist (rather than a doctor or a lawyer, like most other immigrant Jews) to his mother's way of greeting him after school. While most Jewish mothers asked their children, 'Did you learn anything today?' Rabi's mother asked him, 'Did you ask any good questions today?'[6]

The ability to ask questions also implies the ability to listen well, which is a particular feature of vocational discernment that lies at the heart of Christian spirituality. This will now be explored through the particular lenses of Benedict, Ignatius Loyola and the Religious Society of Friends, whose insights have particular relevance for spiritual leadership.

Benedictine spirituality

St Benedict (died 547) formed a lay monastic community where his 'Rule', or way of community life, was first used. 'It has continued in daily use through the fourteen centuries since St Benedict in Monte Cassino first gave it to his monks to help them in their desire to follow Christ more faithfully.'[7] Through his Rule, Benedict was seeking to establish 'a school for the Lord's service'.[8] The prime command of the Rule is to listen. Echoing

---

5 Laura Chasin, 'Searching for Wise Questions', available at http://www.publicconversa tions.org/resources/searching-wise-questions (accessed 21st May 2011).

6 The full article is available at http://www.forward.com/articles/3565/ (accessed 21st May 2011).

7 P. Barry, 2004, *Saint Benedict's Rule*, Mahwah, NJ: HiddenSpring.

8 Barry, *Saint Benedict's Rule*, ch. 8.

Proverbs 1.8, the Rule begins 'Listen, child of God, to the guidance of your teacher. Attend to the message you hear and make sure it pierces to your heart, so that you may accept with willing freedom, and fulfill by the way you live, the directions that come from your loving Father.'[9] The disposition of listening is one that is inquisitive, open to learn and change.

Monks are expected to display obedience to the abbot, but in turn, the abbot has a duty to listen to the advice of the whole community on matters of importance 'because it often happens that the Lord makes the best course clear to one of the younger members'.[10] Abbots are chosen both for their wisdom and experience (that is what they know) and their vulnerability (that is their openness to listen and learn from others).

Ignatian spirituality

Ignatius Loyola (died 1556) was the founder of the Society of Jesus, better known as the Jesuits. Ignatian spirituality is widely studied but frequently misunderstood. It is known for its imaginative meditation on Scripture, for individually guided retreats and for the Spiritual Exercises which are all seen as ways of deepening an individual's relationship with God. This is true but misses the essential point that the purpose of Ignatian spirituality is primarily to enable individuals to play their part with others in making the world a better place by living active Christian lives of useful service. The Jesuits are a missional order not a settled community and so the Ignatian processes are means to an end not, as seems the case for some today, ends in their own right.

Vocational discernment lies at the heart of Ignatian spirituality which is discovered through an ever deepening awareness of God's grace and limitless love that provides the security for us to be properly detached or 'indifferent' to other forces that seek to control us (including cultures, families, possessions and ambitions) so that we might be entirely free to do God's will. All the processes that Ignatius uses in the Spiritual Exercises invite a continually questioning and reflective stance before God. This is focused in the discipline of the *examen* which provides structured questions to reflect on the experiences of the day, to notice our emotional response (How did I feel when that happened?), to discern God's activity (Where did I see God at work? What did he say?) and so make choices for future activity.

Unlike Benedictine spirituality, which has provided much inspiration for contemporary writers on both Christian and business leadership, Ignatius has been largely ignored in this respect. One notable exception is

---

9 Barry, *Saint Benedict's Rule*, Prologue.
10 Barry, *Saint Benedict's Rule*, ch. 3.

the work of Chris Lowney, whose book *Heroic Leadership*[11] draws compelling parallels between leadership in today's business world and Ignatian spirituality. He describes four practices or values of an Ignatian-inspired leader: self-awareness, ingenuity, love and heroism.

Self-awareness is the foundation, and corresponds to the preparation provided by the Spiritual Exercises. Innovation concerns the confident adaptation to a changing world.

> Loyola described the ideal Jesuit as 'living with one foot raised' – always ready to respond to emerging opportunities . . . A leader must rid him- or herself of ingrained habits, prejudices, cultural preferences, and the 'we've always done it this way' attitude – the baggage that blocks rapid adaptive responses. Of course, not *everything* is discardable baggage. Core beliefs and values are nonnegotiable, the centering anchor that allows for purposeful change as opposed to aimless drifting on shifting currents. The leader adapts confidently by knowing what's negotiable and what isn't.[12]

The practice of love concerns the leader's attitude to themselves and others as members of a worldwide community. The final principle is that of heroism. Loyola called his followers to 'elicit great desires' with the 'motto, *magis*, the idea that there is always something more, something greater'.[13] This is a proactive stance that helps leaders 'extract gold from the opportunities at hand rather than waiting for golden opportunities to be handed to them'.[14] But this is not about creating a single heroic leader but rather a team of individually and mutually motivated leaders with a commitment to risk taking; to contribute meaningfully beyond their own interests; to delegate boldly; and to inspire others to turn corporate aspiration into personal mission.

Lowney claims that these values or ways of working 'form an integrated, self-reinforcing whole, or as the Jesuits called it, a *modo de proceder*'.[15] Working around this virtuous circle requires a social community where partnership with other people is the model for learning and action, as the self-development of a leader cannot be done in isolation. This fosters interdependence and mutual care and results in a real commitment to team working. All Jesuits have the same spiritual preparation and so common values and practices can be taken for granted rather than having to be developed in the formation of each new team. However, Jesuits are

---

11 C. Lowney, 2003, *Heroic Leadership*, Chicago: Loyola Press.
12 Lowney, *Heroic Leadership*, p. 29.
13 Lowney, *Heroic Leadership*, p. 34.
14 Lowney, *Heroic Leadership*, p. 33.
15 Lowney, *Heroic Leadership*, p. 245.

not dependent on teams, their individual motivation and clarity of vocation means that they can act alone or with others. Their spiritual disciplines, especially the *examen*, give them a resilience that can keep them focused in times of difficulty or isolation.

So, unlike Benedictine spirituality, where the focus is on on-going formation in a stable Christian community, the Ignatian emphasis is on thorough preparation of the individual, through the Spiritual Exercises, before beginning to fulfil one's vocation which might be with other Jesuits or alone (but always in relationship with or under supervision by other Jesuits). Both traditions value questions and give emphasis to discernment and theological reflection. Both traditions are needed in today's Church, which seeks to offer a stable community of care and nurture and to be working beyond the church community in mission.

Quakerism

Parker Palmer suggests that Quakerism is a tradition 'where they know how to come together in support of people engaged in deep inner work. They come together in a way that is supportive but not invasive, that asks a lot of probing questions but never renders judgment or gives advice . . . in a way that respects the mystery of the human heart but still allows people to challenge and stretch one another in that mystery.'[16] This questioning and supportive disposition is attractive and applicable in both discernment and conflict resolution processes.

An important Quaker process is that of 'Friendly Disentangling' as a means of moving towards win–win solutions to problems. The process has four principles:

The basic principle is that there is something of good, and thus of God, in everyone. This is considered to be one of the most important principles of Quakerism as stated by one of its founders, George Fox: 'Walk cheerfully over the face of the earth answering that of Go(o)d in everyone.'[17] This provides a positive starting point; it looks for the best motivation and behaviour in the other and assumes that there is some common good to be discovered.

The second principle is that people are the product of their social contexts so that 'individual behaviors and values are greatly influenced by the tradition systems within which they are born and socialized. Further, there can be contradictions and dysfunctionalities among entangled system

16 P. J. Palmer, 1998, 'Leading from Within', in L. C. Spears (ed.), *Insights on Leadership*, New York, NY: John Wiley, p. 207.

17 R. P. Nielson, 'Quaker Foundations for Greenleaf's Servant Leadership', in Spears (ed.), *Insights on Leadership*, p. 135.

tradition components and that of Go(o)d in everyone.'[18] In other words, it will help in disputes to look beyond the personal to the systemic thinking and behaviour that has enculturated the individual and to recognize that this enculturation has multiple, often contradictory, sources, some of which may be 'oppressive' and harmful.

The third principle is, for both ethical and effectiveness reasons, to act in a friendly and cheerful manner with all those we may be in conflict with.

The final principle is to try things out on the journey towards a solution, not to wait for the perfect answer.

> A key component of the Quaker method is that experimentation needs to be continuing. There will always be mixtures of the good and the less good, entanglements of the good with oppressive biases and customs. As one set of biases and entanglements appear and are more or less solved, other biases and entanglements emerge . . . There is a continuing opportunity and need for cocreation, leadership, and problem solving with 'that of Go(o)d in everyone'.[19]

At its heart, 'Friendly Disentangling' encourages a questioning, learning disposition in order to solve problems and move forward with integrity and consensus.

Culture and organizations

We now move from the personal and the spiritual to look at the importance of organizational culture. Clergy often work with multiple organizational cultures. In the Church of England, they are normally the primary leader within a local church, congregation or parish; they will be part of a deanery (a small geographic grouping of parishes); part of a diocese (a larger geographic area centred on a bishop and cathedral) and also part of the national Church of England and worldwide Anglican Communion. A leader's role is to help shape and reshape organizations to meet their purpose and mission. For the Church of England, at whatever level, this is ultimately about the *Missio Dei* and the transformation of individuals and society. The organizational development researcher Edgar Schein puts it like this:

> I believe that cultures begin with leaders who impose their own values and assumptions on a group. If that group is successful and the assumptions

18 Nielson, 'Quaker Foundations', p. 136.
19 Nielson, 'Quaker Foundations', p. 138.

come to be taken for granted, we then have a culture that will define for later generations of members what kinds of leadership are acceptable. The culture now defines leadership. But as the group runs into adaptive difficulties, as its environment changes to the point where some of its assumptions are no longer valid, leaders come into play once more. Leadership is now the ability to perceive the limitations of one's own culture and to evolve the culture adaptively is the essence and ultimate challenge of leadership.[20]

This . . . requires the ability to surmount one's own taken-for-granted assumptions, seeing what is needed to ensure the health and survival of the group, and orchestrating events and processes that enable the group to evolve toward new cultural assumptions. Without leadership in this sense, groups will not be able to adapt to changing environmental conditions.[21]

He identifies three levels of culture. The first is what he calls *artefacts* or the most visible organizational structures and ways of working. These are the things that can be seen, heard or felt. They are symbolic of deeper aspects of the organization's culture and so, although they are easy to observe, they can be ambiguous and hard to understand. Observation is never entirely objective; our perceptions will be shaped by the culture(s) with which we are most familiar and which have shaped us. 'It is especially dangerous to try to infer the deeper assumptions from artefacts alone because one's interpretations will inevitably be projections of one's own feelings and reactions.'[22] I am reminded of the aphorism usually attributed to the Talmud that 'We do not see the world as it is. We see the world as we are.' This is a trap that clergy can fall into during their initial months in a new church by forming opinions and developing plans for change based on surface evidence without examining the underlying motivations, values and assumptions of the congregation. It takes time to really understand a new culture and to recognize its similarities with, and differences from, the church cultures we have experienced in the past and come to consider as normal.

At the next level of culture are the organization's *espoused values*, their strategies, goals and philosophies. These are first shaped by the organization's founder and assimilated as 'the way we do things round here'. The deepest level of culture relates to the organization's *basic underlying assumptions*, which are formed in reaction to positive experiences. These

---

20 E. H. Schein, 2004, *Organizational Culture and Leadership*, San Francisco, CA: Jossey-Bass, p. 2.
21 Schein, *Organizational Culture*, p. 414.
22 Schein, *Organizational Culture*, p. 27.

assumptions become implicit over time and can be hard to surface. Schein says that 'When a solution to a problem works repeatedly, it comes to be taken for granted. What was once a hypothesis, supported only by a hunch or a value, comes gradually to be treated as a reality. We come to believe that nature really works this way.'[23]

One way to understand an organization's culture is to try to change it! A change in praxis or policy at the two highest levels of culture may be unproblematic providing no underlying assumptions are challenged. On the other hand, a seemingly trivial change which is at variance with the organization's basic assumptions will be resisted with great emotional intensity. Listening to the stories of change in a parish can be very revealing!

Five methods for asking good questions

To conclude this chapter, we will move from a survey of traditions and disciplines to consider five methods of personal and organizational development that are built around the use of questions. Taken together they provide a valuable toolkit for ministerial and church development.

Asking ourselves good questions

Marilee Goldberg[24] has written about the use of questions in short-term therapy and from this has developed a wider application in coaching and other non-therapeutic contexts.[25] In the preface to her substantive work, *The Art of the Question*, Goldberg traces her growing fascination with the use of questions and quotes Rainer Maria Rilke's poem:

> Be patient toward all that is unresolved in your heart.
> Try to love the questions themselves.
> Do not now seek the answers,
> which cannot be given because you would not be able to live them.
> And the point is to live everything.
> Live the question now.
> Perhaps you will then gradually without noticing it,
> Live along some distant day into the answers.[26]

---

23 Schein, *Organizational Culture*, p. 30.
24 Marilee also writes under her married name Adams.
25 See www.inquiryinstitute.com (accessed 21st May 2011).
26 M. Goldberg, 1998, *The Art of the Question: A Guide to Short-Term Question-Centered Therapy*, New York: John Wiley, p. vi.

Goldberg comes to the conclusion that questions, rather than statements, are the way to alter circumstances and that 'a powerful question alters all thinking and behaving that occurs afterwards' so that 'a question not asked is a door not opened'.[27] As a result, she encourages everyone to adopt what she calls 'a researcher's nonbiased, non-defensive, solution-seeking mindset'.[28] She offers a basic set of questions to encourage this stance, which are:

What do I want?
What are my choices?
What assumptions am I making?
What am I responsible for?
How else can I think about this?
What is the other person thinking, feeling, needing, and wanting?
What am I missing or avoiding?
What can I learn . . . from this person or situation?
                . . . from this mistake or failure?
                . . . from this success?
What questions should I ask (myself or others?)
What action steps make the most sense?
How can I turn this into a win–win?
What is possible?[29]

The heart of Goldberg's work is her choice model, which identifies the source of human response as coming from either our *Judger Self* or our *Learner Self*. The Judger Self refers to that part of us that is 'inflexible, problem-focused, past-oriented, and reactive. It tends to be blame-seeking . . . The Judger Self part of us typically asks questions such as: *"Who or what is wrong?" "Who, or what, is to blame?" "How could I get hurt?" "How can I protect myself?" "How can I win (regardless of the other person)?"* and *"Why does this always happen to me?"'*[30] In contrast, the Learner Self refers to that part of us that is 'open-minded, flexible, responsive, solution-seeking, future-facing, and accepting of self and others. The Learner Self makes *active choices*, being aware that it chooses how to respond in any moment . . . [their questions] include: *"What's going on here?" "What can*

---

27 Goldberg, *The Art of the Question*, p. ix.

28 Goldberg, *The Art of the Question*, p. 11.

29 This version of the questions is taken from http://inquiryinstitute.com/resources/top-12-questions/ (accessed 21st May 2011) and is a development of the questions offered on p. 11 of Goldberg's book.

30 Goldberg, *The Art of the Question*, p. 68.

I learn from it?" "In what ways might this be useful?" . . . "What's the best thing to do now?" "How can we resolve this to our mutual satisfaction?"[31] A biblical example of this is provided by Peter in Acts 10.9–20 where his conversation with the 'voice' in his vision enabled him to transcend his tradition and follow the Spirit's prompting to share the gospel with gentiles.

Goldberg goes on to identify a *Skilful Learner Self* which accepts that the Judger part of the self is always present and can make a positive or shadow contribution in everyone. 'The ever present possibility of the Judger swinging into action keeps the skillful Learner alert, and present focused.'[32]

Goldberg's model is presented as a map, as shown in Figure 1. The map invites *observation* – which path am I on and is it the right one for this context? If we can observe that we are following the Judger path, it is more likely that we can choose to start asking Learner questions in order to join the responsive path of the Learner Self.

Figure 1. Marilee Goldberg's Choice Map[33]

31 Goldberg, *The Art of the Question*, pp. 68–9.
32 Goldberg, *The Art of the Question*, p. 69.
33 Based on Figure 4.1 in Goldberg. This version copied from www.arlingtonva.us/Departments/CPHD/Documents/11389Choice%20Map%2007%200524.pdf (accessed 21st May 2011).

Coaching

Simply asking ourselves questions may not be enough to escape from our own cherished paradigms and mindsets. Coaching provides a powerful method of working with another person and is well described in Jenny Rogers' book *Coaching Skills*. For her, the aim of coaching is to 'facilitate learning for the client'[34] through developing self-awareness. This sets the context for coaching as an equal relationship between two individuals where the coach assists the client to implement practical solutions to their issues or problems. It differs from mentoring which has overtones of an older, wiser, more senior person passing on wisdom and advice to a less experienced, junior colleague. It differs from some forms of therapy in that it is focused on the present and future, not in dealing with the past.

Coaching makes use of a variety of skills including attentive listening, creating rapport, and challenging, but asking the right questions, at the right time, is at the heart of it. Rogers offers a set of 16 'super useful' questions that are content free, short, and facilitate a journey from 'the client stating the problem, going on to restating the problem as a goal, then to naming options and finally to first steps to action'.[35] Her questions are:

What's the issue?
What makes it an issue now?
Who owns this issue/problem?
How important is it on a 1–10 scale?
How much energy do you have for a solution on a 1–10 scale?
What have you already tried?
Imagine the problem's been solved, what would you see, hear and feel?
What's standing in the way of that ideal outcome?
What's your own responsibility for what's been happening?
What early signs are there that things might be getting better/going all right?
Imagine you are at your most resourceful. What do you say to yourself about the issue?
What are the options for action here?
What criteria will you use to judge the options?
Which option seems the best one against these criteria?
So, what's the next/first step?
When will you take it?[36]

---

34 J. Rogers, 2004, *Coaching Skills*, Maidenhead: Open University Press, p. 80.
35 Rogers, *Coaching Skills*, p. 66.
36 Rogers, *Coaching Skills*, pp. 67–8.

Coaching is now very widespread in the commercial world and there may well be people in local congregations who would offer you some coaching sessions.

Spiritual direction

Spiritual direction is another client-centred relationship between two people. It differs from coaching in that it is usually longer-term and not aimed at problem solving, but is similar in being focused on the present and future rather than the past. It has a specific religious context and includes theological reflection and vocational discernment. One definition of spiritual direction is

> help given by one Christian to another which enables that person to pay attention to God's personal communication to him or her, to respond to this personally communicating God, to grow in intimacy with this God, and to live out the consequences of the relationship. The focus of this type of spiritual direction is on experience, not ideas, and specifically on religious experience.[37]

At the heart of spiritual direction is the exploration of five questions:

- *What* has been happening?
- *How* have I been affected?
- *How* has God been at work in the situation?
- *What* biblical and spiritual resources can help me understand all this?
- *How* should I respond and act in the future?

The process differs from coaching in that it will be expected that the spiritual director will have wisdom to offer and resources to suggest. However, this is not done from a position of authority, superiority or power but from a loving commitment to the good of the other and in mutual, prayerful submission to God. Thus the relationship can be seen as a three-way conversation that is dependent on, and enabled by, God the Holy Spirit. The task for the spiritual director is to listen intently in two directions and respond to what is revealed using their gifts, wisdom and insights.

---

37 William A. Barry, SJ and William J. Connolly, SJ in *The Practice of Spiritual Direction*, quoted with many other definitions at www.sdiworld.org/what_is_spiritual_direction2/what-is-christian-spiritual-direction.html (accessed 21st May 2011).

Spiritual direction is now the norm for Christian leaders and most dioceses or regions have a network of contacts.

Appreciative Inquiry

Appreciative Inquiry[38] is a deceptively simple method that comes from the world of organization development and is based on research which shows that organizations make better progress when they focus on and develop their strengths instead of trying to overcome their problems and weaknesses. And so, Appreciative Inquiry (AI) begins with the positive and asks what is life-giving that deserves to be valued and carried forward into the future.

AI has been used widely in the Roman Catholic Church and commended with these words from Pope John XXIII: 'Consult not your fears, but your hopes and dreams. Think not about your frustrations, but about your unfulfilled potential. Concern yourself not with what you tried and failed in, but with what it is still possible for you to do.'[39]

The long-term use of AI in one congregation is best described by Mark Branson.[40] Even if the full AI process is not used, the initial stage can be of great help in uncovering organizational culture and values as it invites people to tell their stories of their best involvement with the Church.

Why not have a go at asking a few people in your church the following three groups of questions:

1. Reflecting on your entire experience at our church, remember a time when you felt most engaged, alive and motivated. Please tell me the story: Who was involved? What did you do? How did it feel? What happened?
2. So from what you have said, what do you value most about our church? What activities or ingredients or ways of life are most important? What are the best features of this church?
3. Finally, if you could make three wishes for the future of our church, what would they be? What might the church look like as these wishes come true?

---

38 For further AI resources see http://appreciativeinquiry.case.edu/ including an accessible introduction to Appreciative Inquiry at http://appreciativeinquiry.case.edu/uploads/whatisai.pdf (accessed 21st May 2011).

39 S. S. Paddock, 2003, *Appreciative Inquiry in the Catholic Church*, Plano, TX: Thin Book.

40 M. L. Branson, 2004. *Memories, Hopes, and Conversations: Appreciative Inquiry and Congregational Change*, Herndon, VA: Alban Institute.

These open and positive questions enable others to tell their stories without producing the usual list of complaints about what is wrong with the church or unrealistic 'if only . . .' statements. Untold stories will tend to lock us in the past, longing for some supposed 'golden-age' or for healing from past hurts. But the simple act of telling our best stories to another human being who wants to listen both builds relationships (and thus a community of trust) and entices us to want to create new stories together about a positive future. AI is a great tool for church leaders to build understanding and trust but it has to be used face-to-face. One church leader I know asks the basic three questions at every pastoral visit he makes and the depth of knowledge and relationship he has now built up has enabled quick and successful development to take place without dissent.

Action Learning

Our final questioning method moves from one-to-one work to learning together with a group of peers. It has sometimes been described as group coaching and could be seen as a particular form of theological reflection group.

Chris Argyris is a frequently cited author in the field of organizational development and especially in connection with adult learning.[41] He coined the terms *single-loop* and *double-loop* learning to distinguish between mere problem solving, which focuses on making changes or fixing problems in the external environment, and a more critical, reflective process that identifies ways in which our own behaviour inadvertently contributes to organizational problems. Without double-loop learning, the way in which we define and solve problems can itself be a source of problems.[42]

Argyris points to research he has done with professional consultants, whom he assumed would be good at learning. However, the reality was very different. He found that highly skilled professionals are very good at single-loop learning and can apply their knowledge to solve problems. But if these solutions fail, the likelihood is they will become defensive and blame others rather than reflect on their own behaviour and contribution to the problem. The very people whose role is to help others learn

41 For a helpful summary of his life and work, see M. K. Smith, 2001, 'Chris Argyris: theories of action, double-loop learning and organizational learning', *The Encyclopedia of Informal Education*, www.infed.org/thinkers/argyris.htm (accessed 21st May 2011).
42 C. Argyris, 2006, 'Teaching Smart People How to Learn', in J. V. Gallos (ed.), *Organization Development*, San Francisco, CA: Jossey-Bass.

76

are often those who block their own and others' learning. I fear that the traditional means of educating and forming clergy have resulted in just this tendency in many ministers! Action Learning[43] is a powerful way to overcome this problem.

Action Learning Groups (sometimes called *Sets*) assist their members to become more effective in achieving useful action, i.e. developing the most appropriate behaviour in each particular situational context. The groups work with one member's real-life situation at a time so learning can be directly applied and as each group member participates all are helped to learn and grow. At its simplest an Action Learning Group works like this: one member describes a problem or issue that they are currently facing; having described the issue (without interruption), other members ask questions to clarify their understanding. Once the issues are sufficiently clear, group members ask coaching-style questions to help the speaker to better understand themselves, the issues and their possible options for action. At the end, the whole group reflects on the process and the next steps the speaker plans to take. These are recorded so that progress can be reported at the next meeting. Often the whole cycle can be completed in 30 to 40 minutes meaning that two or three issues can be tackled in each meeting of the group.

Usually the hardest aspect of Action Learning concerns formulating appropriate questions and resisting the temptation to give advice or share anecdotes (such as 'When that happened to me, I did . . .'). Action Learning Groups can benefit from having a facilitator to get a group going and to periodically review progress.

Conclusion

Ministers and leaders would quickly become annoying and ineffective if their only way of working was through asking questions. Equally, a minister or leader who always proclaims answers with certainty will find it hard to learn and will be ineffective in harnessing all the gifts and abilities of their communities. Like many things, the ideal leader must manage the paradox of competing ways of working, but that is nothing new! St Paul knew all about leaders having strength in weakness, wisdom in unknowing and power in weakness (2 Cor. 12.9–10).

---

43 See http://en.wikipedia.org/wiki/Action_learning and www.actionlearningassociates. co.uk/actionlearning.html (accessed 21st May 2011) for a useful summary of Action Learning's origin and method.

We need both personal discernment and the help of colleagues to know when it is safe to make use of our strengths, skills, wisdom and knowledge or when we should 'empty ourselves', stand back, wait, or let others lead. The key is the mutual recognition that everyone in the community of God is unique, valued, gifted, and in the process of being saved and transformed into the likeness of Jesus. The particular call of the leader is to be listening to God, themselves and the community and offering or withholding their wisdom, gifts and questions in service to both God and the community.

Further reading

Identity, vocation and emotional intelligence

J. Ortberg, 2010, *The Me I Want to Be*, Grand Rapids: Zondervan is a good starting point. A. Hargrave, 2010, *Living Well*, London: SPCK is helpful for developing a personal rule of life and offers good suggestions and resources (see also www.elycathedral.org/worship/spirituality.html).

P. J. Palmer, 1998, 'Leading from Within', in L. C. Spears (ed.), *Insights on Leadership*, New York, NY: John Wiley is of vital importance and can be found at www.couragerenewal.org/parker/writings together with several other articles; an updated version appears in P. J. Palmer, 2000, *Let Your Life Speak: Listening for the Voice of Vocation*, San Francisco: Jossey-Bass.

S. P. Walker, 2007, *Leading out of Who You Are*, Carlisle: Piquant Editions is the first of a series exploring the very important concept of undefended leadership; see also www.theleadershipcommunity.webeden.co.uk.

Despite the title, M. E. Seligman, 2003, *Authentic Happiness: Using the New Positive Psychology to Realise Your Potential for Lasting Fulfilment*, London: Nicholas Brealey Publishing is well worth reading. Also good is M. Buckingham and D. Clifton, 2002, *Now, Discover Your Strengths*, London: Simon and Schuster, which includes a code to use Gallup's StrengthsFinder® (so don't buy a used copy!). For other strengths-based/authentic happiness surveys see www.authentichappiness.sas.upenn.edu/questionnaires.aspx.

Daniel Goleman brought the idea of Emotional Intelligence to popularity, see for example D. Goleman, 1988, *Working with Emotional Intelligence*, London: Bloomsbury; especially recommended as an accessible UK introduction with resources for developing EQ is A. Bacon and

A. Dawson, 2010, *Emotional Intelligence for Rookies*, London: Marshall Cavendish. The tiny M. Chapman, 2001, *Emotional Intelligence Pocketbook,* Alresford: Management Pocketbooks is also helpful. For web resources see http://www.cipd.co.uk/subjects/lrnanddev/selfdev/emotintel.htm, http://en.wikipedia.org/wiki/Emotional_intelligence and http://www.businessballs.com/eq.htm.

Thinking and reflecting skills

N. Kline, 1999, *Time to Think*, London: Cassell Illustrated is highly recommended. R. Walton, 2012, *The Reflective Disciple*, London: SCM Press is firmly related to Christian growth.

Learning, Using Questions and Developing People

C. Edmondson, 2010, *Leaders Learning to Listen*, London: Darton, Longman and Todd is an excellent introduction.

For resources on the power and use of questions, see M. Goldberg, 1998, *The Art of the Question: A Guide to Short-Term Question-Centered Therapy*, New York: John Wiley and the author's website at www.inquiryinstitute.com. M. J. Marquardt, 2005, *Leading with Questions*, San Francisco, CA: Jossey-Bass is recommended.

For resources on spiritual direction see M. Guenther, 1992, *Holy Listening: The Art of Spiritual Direction*, London: Darton, Longman and Todd; S. Pickering, 2008, *Spiritual Direction*, London: Canterbury Press; and, for non-specialist parish clergy, D. R. Bidwell, 2004, *Short-Term Spiritual Guidance*, Minneapolis: Augsburg Fortress. Spiritual direction is usually regarded as a one-to-one ministry, but can be done very effectively in a group; one of the few resources for this that I have come across is R. M. Dougherty, 1995, *Group Spiritual Direction*, Mahwah, NJ: Paulist Press.

Good books on coaching include J. Rogers, 2004, *Coaching Skills*, Maidenhead: Open University Press and D. Megginson and D. Clutterbuck, 2005, *Techniques for Coaching and Mentoring*, Oxford: Elsevier. For a specifically Christian approach see R. Melander, 2006, *A Generous Presence: Spiritual Leadership and the Art of Coaching*, Herndon, VA: Alban Institute.

Two excellent reference works are P. Hawkins and N. Smith, 2006, *Coaching, Mentoring and Organizational Consultancy: Supervision and Development*, Maidenhead: Open University Press, and A. Brockbank and

I. McGill, 2006, *Facilitating Reflective Learning through Mentoring and Coaching*, London: Kogan Page.

J. A. Raelin, 2008, *Work-Based Learning: Bridging Knowledge and Action in the Workplace*, San Francisco: Jossey-Bass is an excellent reference work offering processes to improve the application of learning in the workplace.

6

Creating Critical Conversations

STUART BURNS

It is not unusual within any training relationship that one party has more experience in critical or theological reflection than the other. In recent years, theological education has developed many methods and models for reflective practice, and theological reflection in particular. Curates can leave college steeped in a model of reflective practice, perceiving this as the norm. Training incumbents can be so linked to the rigours of ministry that their reflection is constrained within a context-specific frame. It is the intention of this chapter to consider how our mutual reflection can be more focused, and to raise awareness of some of the barriers to critical reflection and critical conversations that can occur within the training context. Hopefully, I will provide a framework, and a language that allows our experiences to be articulated, and our individual assumptions and expectations in our reflection to be surfaced.

Reflective practices: in, on, for

Reflective practice involves making sense of events, situations or actions and emphasizes the importance of a thoughtful and prayerful approach to understanding experience. This is the process by which we draw on existing ideas and understanding, and in applying them to our experience, we may either confirm these ideas or develop new ones. If reflection stems from engagement with both experience and theory, then theological reflection is simply giving attention and consideration to experience and theory while listening to God at the same time, leading to an evaluating and discerning of our sense-making against our faith and mission.

The time perspective of our reflection is important – not all reflective practice takes place in the safety of the study, or retreat house! There are three chronologies of reflection. Reflection can be real time (Reflection-In-Action), retrospective (Reflection-On-Action) and also future focused (Reflection-For-Action). Of these three Reflection-On-Action is the most common in ministerial training. However, an awareness of the influence of Reflection-For-Action is crucial to any critical conversation. Reflection-For-Action brings a nuance to our understanding of real-time or retrospective reflection – particularly to the person in the position of trainee. It gives a thoughtful approach to expectations and motivations, and allows us to rehearse role and orientation. It allows the question of future engagement and action to be raised. In the case of a student in training, either as a minister or youth worker, there is the engagement of prior experience (On Action), current experience in hand (In Action), and also of presumed experience to come (For Action). This is true of those in courses or colleges, and also within the first years of any appointment, such as IME 4–7, or a probationary ministerial placement. The influence of 'presumed experience' is not new. It was initially articulated by Donald Schön in 1971, and latterly through the work of Peter Senge.[1] Schön spoke of it as a future 'stable state'.

> I have believed for as long as I can remember in an afterlife within my own life – a calm, stable state to be reached after a time of troubles. When I was a child, that afterlife was Being Grown Up. As I have grown older, its content has become more nebulous, but the image of it stubbornly persists.[2]

The stable state never arrives, yet it pervades our thinking, our planning and our training – and our reflections. Any organization that looks to the future from the perspective of the present can be in search of a stable state. It exists in the personal domain, when 'things have settled down', 'the kids have left home', 'the partner has been found' or the 'health has been recovered'. The 'search for the stable state is found in both voluntary organizations and commercial businesses – when 'the current recession is over', 'the budget is met' or 'the sales have begun'. In churches it becomes evident from the micro 'after Sunday' or the yearning for 'Ordinary Time', to the 'building project completed' or 'when the outreach is finished'. But more so – in our training and development of ministers, we formalize and institutionalize this search. What is selection and training

---

1 Donald Schön, 1971, *Beyond the Stable State*, New York: Norton and Peter M. Senge, 2006, *The Fifth Discipline: The Art and Practice of the Learning Organization*, New York: Random House.
2 Schön, *Beyond the Stable State*, p. 9.

for ministry without a search for a stable state? 'When I am selected', 'when I am licensed', 'when I am ordained', 'when I am a priest', when I have my own church' or even, 'when I have accomplished all my competency requirements'.

The search is not the issue. Within the Christian faith the belief that one day soon 'all will be well' is a common motif. Consider the understanding of transformation, of moving 'from glory to glory' (2 Cor. 3.18, AV) of climbing the Ladder of Divine Ascent, of the progress of the believer to be more Christ-like, not to mention the Pauline eschatological 'now and not yet' of the Christian life. This is the stuff to which we cling, and to which we aspire. Such journeying is not smooth, or one directional. Nor should it be. But the stubbornly persistent ideal stable state will always remain out of reach, and can divert our energies, our passions, our mission and our ministry, our creativity and our reflection, to the point of us avoiding the learning, of neglecting the journey, and of unquestioningly accepting the status quo. If our ministry is prone to this search, ministerial training can be paralysed by it, and reflective practice weakened. If the stable state potentially focuses our reflection towards the 'presumed experience to come', the need then is for reflective practice (Reflection-For-Action) that is both timely and critical. That is, practice that allows engagement with the real-time and the retrospective, and still illuminates the future without being constrained by the expectations and assumptions of any long-term training programme.

Reflection and theory

Alongside the chronology reflection of In/On/For, we need to consider the content of our reflections and conversations. A useful categorization, by Burgoyne and Reynolds, suggests three types of reflective practice.[3]

Effective Practice (EP) Refers to reflection that focuses upon the effective, and the performance. EP practitioners are those who know they perform, but may regard their skill as intuitive, unconscious, tacit. (*Questions such as How do I do this?*)

Reflective Practice (RP) Refers to reflection that focuses upon the working theory of practice, in that it suggests what should be done and why

---

3 J. Burgoyne and Michael Reynolds, 1997, *Management Learning*, London: Sage.

it should work. This is reflection and practice that will become and remain normative. (*Questions such as How can I do this better? What do I bring to this?*)

Critically Reflective Practice (CRP) Refers to reflection that questions and challenges the presuppositions. Critically reflective practitioners operate in what they judge to be the best 'working idea' available to them at all times, but they also have a commitment continually to search for a better one. (*Questions such as Why am I doing this? Why is the institution doing it this way?*)

Burgoyne and Reynolds assert that the critically reflective practitioner has access to the most sophisticated process of learning that we are capable of, given our current state of understanding. Critically Reflective Practice builds upon the concept of reflection as an integral part of the learning experience. It is different from Reflective Practice. This difference is found through the process of questioning and unmasking of often hidden assumptions, and the grounding of reflection within critical theory rather than problem solving and active experimentation. Critical theory challenges taken-for-granted ways of knowing; to ask not only what is, but who currently benefits, and what are the possible alternatives.[4]

Theology and critical theory

It is important to note that theology (and practical theology in particular) is assisted by critical theory but is not defined by it. Certainly theological reflection is more than critical reflexivity.[5] However, both are mutually tasked to explore and interpret the human condition, and provide a framework for exploration, engagement and reflection. Within reflection, what distinguishes the critically reflective practitioner from the reflective practitioner is the critical theories which allow the claims, assumptions,

---

4 The background to critical theory includes the development of critical theory in education through the work of John Dewey and Peter Jarvis, who draw from the Frankfurt school (particularly Habermas) and the constructs of judgement and discernment. Burgoyne and Trehan have integrated critical theory into the field of Management Learning and Leadership, with particular reference to organizational development, and Small and Medium Enterprises.

5 John Swinton and Harriett Mowatt, 2006, *Practical Theology and Qualitative Research*, London: SCM Press.

contradictions, omissions and value judgements that are built into normative, descriptive and interpretative theories within reflection to be questioned and confronted.[6] It gives opportunity to question the presupposition, to surface the inequality, to discern the hidden voice. It surfaces issues of power, politics and emotion that are otherwise difficult to engage with. Critically Reflective Practice asks questions of the institution, as well as the individual (of the parish as well as the curate!) and requires both an inward looking at our thoughts, and an outward view of the situation or experience.

Within the field of theology and ministry, Critical Reflective Practice often involves a fresh reading of Scripture, and of allowing Scripture to craft our formation and discipleship, rather than unquestioningly reinforce our pre-formed understandings of power, politics and emotion within our faith. It is gospel-orientated in the best tradition, as it allows us to simply ask, 'What light does the gospel shed upon this? What gospel truth is illuminated through this?' It involves asking the questions, as well as listening to the narratives, of individuals and congregations. It relates to hermeneutics and reader response, it engages with Scripture and culture. If used well, it keeps mission central.

Creating critical conversations

Within experiential learning programmes such as IME 1–7, or vocational courses whether individual or organizational, intentional conversations that are based on individual or group experiences form the basis for development and learning. Within training for ministry these intentional conversations occur frequently. Within church life they do occur, but often need to be unearthed from their context – sometimes structured, sometimes opportunistic, but always having the potential for reflection, learning and development. The challenge for those in any development programme or church community is to create space, time and opportunity for those intentional conversations to occur, and for those conversations to move beyond the Effective Practice, and towards the Critically Reflective Practice.

Critical reflection often connects with an unsettling or an insecurity regarding basic assumptions, and the way in which we view ourselves

---

6 Burgoyne, *Management Learning*, p. 4 and Michael Crotty, 1998, *The Foundations of Social Research: Meaning and Perspective in the Research Process*, London: Sage, p. 112f.

and those around us. In practical learning terms this can be regarded as being 'struck' – the spontaneous response to the events or relationships occurring around us. What distinguishes Critically Reflective from merely Reflective Practice is this sense of insecurity. It is why you don't know where you are when you join a college or a course, why you yearn for your previous experience to be taken seriously and credited as valid. Why, when you move between posts, the temptation to recreate a previous pattern of ministry is strong. A curate recounted the experience of beginning a curacy and engaging in parish ministry for the first time as a member of clergy, and realizing that they were being treated differently to their previous experience of full-time ministry. The difficulty is in isolating the unsettling moment or planning the impact within any development programme. In many ways this is unachievable, as realistically no individual or organizational learning education programme can be planned around the *impact* or *unsettling* of any intervention, only the *intent* of the intervention, together with an encouragement to criticality. For example, Schön's *Search for the Stable State* is littered with these moments that have the potential for impact or unsettling, but whose value and opportunity is removed by the fictional stable state. Equally, the trend in ministerial development towards learning outcomes and competencies that require evidence of completion before any appointment can be made reinforces the permanence of the stable state, and endemically weakens the potential for reflection and emancipation. The danger is that the competency emphasis focuses upon the Effective Practice, occasionally releases Reflective Practice, but does not allow time, or opportunity for engagement in any Critical Reflective Practice. However, the opportunity for development and challenge to assumptions and expectations within training is present, although often missed. A curate and training incumbent who minister in a rural context have spoken of the opportunities for Critical Reflective Practice on the return journey from the crematorium – a journey time of some 45 minutes. Of course, the limiting factor to this opportunity is Effective Practice itself – as soon as the curate is competent to conduct a funeral alone, the car journey becomes a solitary activity, and the reflection personal. However, other opportunities abound. In particular IME 1–7 is structured around what the sociologist Peter Jarvis terms 'learning disjuncture'. IME 1–7 has identifiable hidden teachable moments, the unsettlings or the points of being struck. These include formal transition points, from any selection/interview process, to initial training in a college or on a course, as well as training in situ in a parish or local church.

Learning disjunctures

Learning disjunctures are when our biography and the meaning we give to our experience of a social situation are not in harmony and are within two aspects. First, when I cannot give meaning to the sensation that I have, and second, when I do not know the meaning those around me give it. Learning disjunctures can be identified as the gap between our biography and our perception, and either the small adjustments we make to accommodate this, or an identifiable gap within this that requires larger learning. It is a varied and complex experience, but one that gives opportunity to start our learning processes.[7] It is evident within the formation of clergy and Readers as much as within any formal learning environment. Often it is experienced as being stopped in your tracks, because we don't know automatically what to do or how to respond to a question. It is in many ways the teachable moment. The skill in formational development, required from both course and college tutors, as well as training incumbents, IME 4–7 officers and year tutors, is in using these moments to best effect. This is partly about recognizing the moment is there, and partly about intentionally using that opportune moment for a critical conversation. The danger, as Linda Perriton notes, is that every day our reflective questioning grows more akin to that of simply effective training rather than emancipation or releasing.[8] All too often we miss the moment.

What then can we offer as a means to create and locate critical conversations? I offer two tools that can be used as a means to evaluating our current practice, and aligning future conversations to a more creative critical engagement.

A reflective grid

The three categories given by Burgoyne and Reynolds can be combined with the Reflection In/On/For Action by the following grid. The grid illuminates the benefits and challenges of Reflective Practice over and against Reflection In, On and For Action. Thus we are afforded a framework for a conversation, and an opportunity to grapple with the context of our reflection, as well as the context and form.

---

7 Peter Jarvis, 2007, *Globalisation, Lifelong Learning and the Learning Society*, Lifelong Learning and The Learning Society Volume 2, London: Routledge, p. 5.

8 L. Perriton, 2004, 'A Reflection of what exactly? Questioning the Use of "Critical Reflection"', in M. Vince (ed.), *Management Education Contexts: Organising Reflection*, Aldershot: Ashgate, p. 130.

Critically Reflective Practice	Not possible? Can only notice the disconnects	Challenges often. Unsettles	Deeply challenges, requires reframing of intent and assumptions.
Reflective Practice	Reinforces or disturbs	Problem solves. Results in some challenge	Predictive, possibly presumptive. Some practical challenges
Effective Practice	Small practical adjustments	Reinforces practice. Problem solving	Reinforces practice
Initial Experience for Reflection	Reflection-In-Action	Reflection-On-Action	Reflection-For-Action

From this grid, it is suggested that Reflection-In-Action and Critically Reflective Practice are almost incompatible, usually because of time constraints. Similarly, the opportunities afforded by the Reflection-For-Action, Reflective Practice and Critically Reflective Practice are much more accessible and possible, even within a time-constrained training environment. The grid is particularly useful for illuminating and agreeing the basis of the current conversation or reflection, as well as the general pattern of reflective conversations between curate and incumbent. Taking the previous month's reflections and locating them on the grid can provide an opportunity to discuss both the chronology of reflection, as well as the category of reflection offered.

A reflective radio

A reflection image that can be useful for highlighting the required intentionality to create a critical conversation is that of a radio.[9] Any radio needs to be tuned. A radio will not receive a signal without repeated tuning and fine tuning. Signals change in strength and regularity. Sometimes they move purposefully. They respond to pressures in the atmosphere. Rarely will a signal stay in the same place in the same strength for any length of time. Anyone who has sought to find the BBC World Service knows this is a skill to be learnt!

---

9 The initial graphic for the tool was developed in conversations with a colleague in Leicester, Nicky McGinty, and through conversations with training incumbents, curates, first incumbent groups, and colleagues on MAMLL learning sets.

The radio has several elements that can help us reflect and converse, but the original signal is vital. The original signal emanates from the unsettling disjunctured or 'struck' moment, and can be used as the initial event. The event experience may be a pastoral situation that requires thought and reflection before action. It may be a sermon that has been preached, or a decision that has been made. It may be a disagreement, or an encouragement in ministry. It may be church growth and new mission opportunities. The issue is not what the experience or event is, but what we do with it, and how we use the unsettling or learning disjuncture to best potential. In the use of the radio image we recognize that we can tune to different stations, and thus pick up different questions and interpretations of the same experience.

Radios are made to be tuned, and the task we face as users is to tune the radio so that the experience can be reflected upon, and conversations about our learning and ministry can occur. We take the experience, and tune to a station that will bring a clear conversation. Within this model the three radio stations that we tune to whenever we consider our practice and mission are 'Effective Practice', 'Reflective Practice' and 'Critically Reflective Practice', as introduced earlier by Burgoyne, and they are illuminated by effective questions. (See below for examples.)

Effective Practice questions focus upon the immediate responses that let us hear the surface issues. Reflective Practice questions focus upon development and self-awareness and let us hear the strategic issues. Critically Reflective Practice questions focus upon more unsettling questions and let us hear the unsettling themes.

Within the use of the image of the radio, we recognize that assumptions are easily made between two people who want to listen to the same event, but on different stations. For example a curate considering a sermon already preached and the reception it received may be listening to the Effective Practice station, but will become confused if their training incumbent is listening to the Critically Reflective Practice station. One is looking for immediate affirmation; the other is trying to give significant feedback. Misunderstandings arise easily. Assumptions have to be brought to the surface. There has to be an intentional agreement that the participants in the conversation are listening to the same station, for the learning and development to be most useful, honest and developmental. We must move the Event Experience Dial to locate the station that will bring the best quality conversation for those who are gathered. The graphic gives a figurative summary and introduces some of the theories underlying the model.

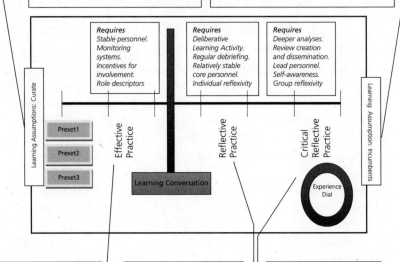

Curate Learning Assumptions & Expectations

What theory of learning influences me most?

What ministry experience do I bring to this? How will these influence me?

What future ministry expectations do I have?

What happened the last time we did this? How successful was it?

Incumbent Learning Assumptions & Expectations

What theory of learning influences me most?

What ministry experience do I bring to this? How will these influence me?

What future ministry expectations do I have?

What happened the last time we did this? How successful was it?

Learning Assumptions: Curate

Requires
Stable personnel.
Monitoring systems.
Incentives for involvement.
Role descriptors

Requires
Deliberative Learning Activity.
Regular debriefing.
Relatively stable core personnel.
Individual reflexivity

Requires
Deeper analyses.
Review creation and dissemination.
Lead personnel.
Self-awareness.
Group reflexivity

Learning Assumption: Incumbents

Preset1
Preset2
Preset3

Effective Practice

Reflective Practice

Critical Reflective Practice

Learning Conversation

Experience Dial

Examples
Self-review.
Experience-based learning
Reflection and immediate feedback.
Immediate incidents.

Examples
Deliberative group verbal learning activity.
Action Learning sets.
Regular Periodic Meetings.
Presentations.
Storytelling.
Reflective journaling.
Critical Incident Analysis.
Reflective metaphors.

Examples
Written analyses, with wide review and agreement.
Critical Action Learning.
Group storytelling.
Group reflective metaphors.
Critical Incident Analysis.

This simple image can be developed to illustrate further the process of creating critical conversations. The process should ideally involve the following stages (questions given are examples, not prescriptive):

1. Assumptions and expectations between participants should be surfaced.
   What stage of training are we now engaged within?
   What unspoken learning styles are influential in this relationship?
   What model of supervision are we each working on?

2. To agree our preset stations.
   Are we each aware of our favourite preset station?
   Do our theological resources reinforce or challenge our engagement?
   Are our presets valid?
   What reflection have you already begun?

3. Identify the unsettling or disjuncture in the experience.
   Present the experience.
   What struck you?
   Did the same things unsettle you both, or are there separate areas for reflection to be agreed?
   Who has brought the unsettling? Whose reflection opportunity is this?
   What meaning are you giving to the unsettling that you experienced?

4. Tune the conversation to the agreed station.
   What method or process of reflection are you going to use?
   Describe the unsettling, or disjuncture.
   Can each listen, and orientate themselves within the experience that is being reflected upon?

5. Ask the key questions that allow learning to surface, rather than assumptions to be reinforced.
   Who cares about this?
   Who can do anything about this?
   Who is privileged in this?
   Who or what is excluded?
   What haven't we noticed?
   What meaning are you giving to this?
   What meaning are others giving to this?
   Is our account valid?

6. Act on the reflection.
   So what?

The difficulties of critical conversations: notes for trainers

Critical reflection is a socially situated, relational, political and collective process. There are three areas of note that show the difficulty and possibility of embedding critical conversations into an existing practice.

First, programme rationale. It cannot be assumed that all that needs to be done is to persuade people to adopt a more critical position in content and approach for creative critical conversations to occur. Critical reflection may encounter resistance, create discomfort, question our theology, and cause conflict with regard to both individual and organizational goals. Inherited models of training are highly influential, and easy to fall back into. Year group facilitators and training incumbents are often expected to support and train rather than critically reflect alongside. To engage in critical conversations in existing programmes and relationships requires clarity of rationale, surfacing of the learning assumptions of participant and facilitator, agreement of organizational learning outcomes and assessments required. For critical reflection to be effective the rationale of emancipation itself needs to be highlighted as concealment of this leads to problems of power and group dynamics as much as the requirements of the overall programme.

Second, public reflection. The role of public reflection is crucial in forming both a community of inquiry and the requirement for learning dialogues within reflection. Critical conversations and a supportive community are not mutually exclusive – indeed, a caring, supportive relationship can distinctly add to reflection when safe presence and trusted peers allow social, political and emotional data to surface. However, group dynamics are such that they must be noted and critical conversations be an agreed, intentional process.

Third, facilitator skill and development. Raelin suggests five key skills of reflective practice that facilitators can successfully model – speaking, disclosing, being, probing, testing.[10] Within this there is a clear need for criticality to remain central, so as to avoid the slippage into Effective Practice or training by becoming reliant upon speaking. If we do not agree it should be critical, reflection may lose its edge. Facilitators and training incumbents need to be trained in the skills of critical reflection. It is an organizational cost that does not necessarily provide immediate observable organizational benefit, and hence is often neglected. Developing the self-perception and cultural awareness of the facilitator through an experience of reflection and emancipation, rather than simply learning a new set

10 J. A. Raelin, 2008, *Work-Based Learning: Bridging Knowledge and Action in the Workplace*, San Francisco: Jossey-Bass, p. 24.

of facilitation rules, is crucial. Learning conversations (as in stage 1 of the radio reflection) prepare for a learning programme. But these conversations need to be a dialogue to establish working consensus as even within the establishment of learning conversations there needs to be an element of criticality and openness. Dialogue in itself is not sufficient to surface assumptions, or to reveal dissonance, and can proscriptively orientate the learning and learner through reinforcement of existing inequalities. It follows that the lead influence within the learning conversation (for example the IME 4–7 officer, year facilitator, or training incumbent) must have a robust rationale for engaging with critical reflection, and be active outside the programme as a critical reflective practitioner as well as facilitator within it. This raises the question as to how we train and develop our training incumbents.

There is a certain irony in that key to releasing the constraining assumptions that are brought to critical reflection is the limiting assumptions of power, politics and emotion in our institutions. The very areas that critical reflection prides itself in surfacing act as a limiting drag anchor to the reflection process. For example, year facilitators can limit the learning of the year group. Emotional conflicts, frustrations and insecurities associated with relations of subordination and subjugation can be silenced, or when they surface, such conflicts are interpreted as problems of individual immaturity and adjustment. Research also shows that 'learning sets', or 'reflection groups', can be used as a subtle means of management control, allowing issues to be raised, but effectively nullifying them through reinforcement of the existing organizational structures or viewpoints.[11] Issues raised in individual critical conversations can have significant ramifications for a parish, church community or wider diocese. The 'So what?' question needs to be addressed by the individual, the group, the parish, and the wider organizational body.

Other writers have already noted the tendency to water down Reflective Practice and simplify its theories, and have also noted how critical learning can be disengaged from reflection. As long ago as 1993, Day was highlighting the tendency for Reflective Practice to be spoken about more than actively engaged with and noting the need for the personal issues that framed the reflection to be made more explicit.[12] As critical reflection

---

11 Claire Rigg and Kiran Trehan, 2009, 'Critical Reflection in the Workplace – Is it just too difficult?', *Journal of European Industrial Training* 32 (5), pp. 374–84 and Hugh Willmott, 1997, 'Making Learning Critical: Identity, Emotion and Power in Process of Management Development', *Systems Practice* 10 (6), pp. 749–71.

12 Peter Day, 1993, 'Reflection: A necessary but not sufficient condition for professional development', *British Educational Journal* 19 (1), pp. 83ff.

moves into the theological and formation environment the dangers of dilution of criticality grow.

Some of the potential shortcomings of critical reflection include

- the tendency to operate within existing managerial agendas and refuse to implement learning revealed by the critical conversation
- to frame change in individualistic and heroic ways
- to become 'isn't it awful' forums that provide psychological support to participants, but do little to address the root causes of organizational problems
- facilitators and leaders being unaware of the consequences of their actions
- the inconsistency gap between our 'espoused theories' and our 'theories-in-use'
- the bias in which individuals obtain information, and the desire to reinforce existing theological positions
- a reliance upon past practices, and a tendency to look for similarities rather than differences
- the necessary vocabulary of critique – without which critical reflection can become lost in a morass of negativity, leading to the derailing of the endeavour
- lack of clarity in both delivery and reception in one-to-one critical conversations
- complex power relations and facilitator/client dissonance.

Creating critical conversations: is it worth the effort?

In the spirit of critical conversations and critical reflection, I should surface my assumption that both critical conversations and reflection can bring individual and organizational insight and significant learning to those involved in ministerial formation. Church and society are moving, culture is changing, and our future ministers need the skills to enquire, challenge, and learn as they minister. Is it worth the effort? Perhaps the question should be: What stops us having critical conversations?

PART 3

Ministry

7

Time Wisdom

STEPHEN CHERRY

Benjamin Franklin famously said that time is money. That's an overstate-
ment but time is like money: the cliché 'you can't take it with you' applies
equally to both. But with time it is even more radical. Every tick of the
clock is the death of the previous second. Time passes. Time flies. No
wonder Old Father Time carries a sickle and undertakers traditionally use
a clock as the sign of their trade. Time and tide 'wait for no man'. People
often think that the saying refers to the ebb and flow of the sea. The reference is actually to the seasons – Christmastide, Eastertide and so on. The
date arrives whether we are ready or not. I recall my first Christmas Eve
in a new parish, or at least about eleven hours of it. There was a three
o'clock Crib Service at one church. Then a six o'clock Christingle Service
at another. I was the first to arrive so I was able to deal with the mess that
drunks had made in the church porch before anyone should be upset by
it. A brief bite to eat, and then I went to visit the family of a parishioner
who had just died. Then it was home to write the sermon before getting
back into church for Midnight Mass, the church being (half) full of people
whom I did not recognize and who did not seem to be very familiar with
Anglican liturgy. When they had all gone home I locked the church door.

Periods of intense activity like this are familiar to people in public ministry. They go with the territory. In some ways, and for some people, they
can be energizing. But on other occasions, or for other people, they can
be quite exhausting. The danger with such episodes, however, is not that
they happen but that whether exhausting or energizing they are exciting or
even slightly intoxicating and after a while they become a way of life: a life
that is busy, rushed, breathless, and all too often self-important and inat-
tentive to the things that really matter. There are several different ways of
reflecting on this reality but in this chapter we are looking at the relationship between ministry and *time*.

Time, as we experience it, has a shape which is both physical and theological. Over many centuries it has been the work of wise Christian schol-
ars and politicians to blend the two together to assist the life-long process

of Christian formation. It is said that when Charles de Foucault went off into the desert he took very little with him but that one key possession was a battered old alarm clock. He needed that to help him shape his days and to say the offices regularly. In doing this he was drawing on a deep monastic intuition. Benedict knew that if you wanted to make space for prayer and spiritual formation, the 'hours' were your friends. And so he organized the day around the hours of prayer and made the 'opus Dei' the number one priority. It focused the community on God and held it together. There were, presumably, many times when members of the community thought all this praying a waste of time. But Benedict, like de Foucault and many holy others, would have appreciated that such 'waste' was fundamental; that they were making time by giving it away. Although that sounds odd, there is theological principle at the heart of it, namely the principle of graceful transformation. That which is given away, or given back to God, is returned with abundance. It is a matter of theological principle that this is true of time.

My liturgical and spiritual home at the time of writing is Durham Cathedral, where there is still a hint of Benedictine attention to detail in our corporate observance of common prayer. That sense of a rhythm that predates any of us and is grounded in both Christian tradition and the cycles of the universe helps support the spirituality of the community and the place and that of each individual person who shares in it. I have myself often reflected on the curious fact that on our way in procession to the stalls for Morning and Evening Prayer we clergy walk under Prior Castell's clock. As we do so, I imagine it skipping forward 25 or so minutes in the morning and three-quarters of an hour in the evening, as if when we enter the next period of time is already spoken for. Those minutes are, you might say, *dedicated*. When we process to the stalls for prayer we step outside the normal time in which we try to get things done efficiently or to engage in our favourite pastimes and step into a world of activities which make sense *only* if there is a world and reality beyond, and deep within, the one of time and space.

Since the Industrial Revolution, human beings have become 'Time Lords'. Not travelling through time, perhaps, but overthrowing some of the limits which our ancestors would have seen as immutable and which their imaginations would have conceived as the boundaries of existence. The creation of machines and devices that can either do work themselves or allow a human being to work much more quickly is something we have taken for granted for generations. We have also taken for granted the increase in life-expectancy which although only recently a cause of worry – who really wants to live for well over a hundred years? – has been increasing at much the same rate for about 200 years. The biblical three score years and ten is no longer seen as a good age and those who do get to four score do not expect to find that 'their strength is but labour and sorrow' (see Psalm 90.10, BCP). Human beings alive in the western world today have far more 'disposable time' than any previous generation could imagine. And yet this is a reality which is rarely celebrated. Indeed any party to celebrate the abundance of free time now on our hands would be drowned out by the chorus of 'time pressure', 'time poverty' and the iconic slogan of the anxiously self-important, 'I'm busy'.

The (a)theology of busyness

The phenomenon, if not the epidemic, of busyness is probably the reason for there being a chapter on time in this book. It is rare to find someone in ministry who does not seek to impress on you just how busy they are. It is a curious business, this busyness, and warrants a good deal more theological reflection than it gets. I doubt whether our ministerial forefathers were given to busyness or that they played a game that I have often observed and which I have, just for fun, dubbed 'diaryopoly'. It begins when a group of clergy need to find a date for a meeting. The first player suggests a date only to be told that it is in the school holidays or half term and so impossible even to consider. Then another date is suggested. One or two innocents declare themselves free to attend, but the more serious players shake their heads sadly, telling us why, although we have not asked, the date is already taken, announcing proudly the significance of the event. And so the dates in the diary become like squares on the Monopoly board. A meeting of school governors might be a house, being invited along to the Bishop's staff that day a bright red hotel. Everyone has to pay their rent in the Monopoly money of resented respect to the busier colleagues. I exaggerate, of course. But there is no status to be had in an empty diary. To fail to be busy is in some way to be seen to fall short of the ministerial mark.

Some clergy are inevitably and objectively busier than others. Those, and there are many of them, whose ministry covers not one or two parishes but three, four, maybe seven or ten. Incumbents of multi-parish benefices can count on the fingers of more than one hand the number of clergy who were ministering across their benefice a generation or so ago. The invention of the motor car, the washing machine, the deep freeze, microwave, word-processor and mobile phone are what makes life possible for these good people. And yet the grand old rectory which stands next to the church outside which they arrive just a few minutes before the service begins (or even some while after a lay colleague has already started the service) speak of a life of privileged, if sometimes down-at-heel, leisure. For their predecessors would have had servants to take the burden out of the day's labours and to ensure that the parson was not distracted from study, care, preaching, prayer and leisured civility.

So it might be, then, that there is a case to be made along the lines that the clergy today really do not have enough time to be able to do everything that needs to be done, never mind everything that is desirable. That is often what people believe when they describe themselves as 'busy'. And yet for Eugene Peterson, at least, this is not a fact of life. In fact, he sees it as a *betrayal*. His words are strong and counter-cultural but need to be heard as we reflect on the relationship between time and ministry. 'The word busy', he writes, 'is the symptom not of commitment but of betrayal. It is not devotion but defection. The adjective "busy" set as a modifier to pastor should sound to our ears like adulterous to characterize a wife or embezzling to describe a banker. It is an outrageous scandal, a blasphemous affront.'[1]

If that is not enough to upset diaryopoly-playing clergy, then his analysis of the spirituality that undergirds such betrayal will certainly light the touch paper. Pastors become busy, he argues, for two 'ignoble' reasons. 'It is either because they are vain or because they are lazy – or both.' I have already made the point about vanity. We make ourselves busy to get the thrill of importance, relevance, and possibly, indispensability. If we have a deep need to be needed then to be needed far beyond our capacity to respond is bliss. It is like being the plumber in a town where everyone's pipes have burst in the frost.

There are many who will find the suggestion that laziness lies at the root of busyness offensive. And yet Peterson calls C. S. Lewis to his defence. Lewis used to argue that only lazy people work hard. Peterson summarizes the point:

> By lazily abdicating the essential work of deciding and directing, establishing values and setting goals, other people do it for us; then we find ourselves frantically, at the last minute, trying to satisfy a half dozen different demands on our time, none of which is essential to our vocation, to stave off the disaster of disappointing someone.[2]

I recall a conversation that I had when was a 'busy incumbent'. My interlocutor said to me 'You know, Stephen, every morning I have to ask myself,

---

1 Eugene Peterson, 1989, *The Contemplative Pastor*, Grand Rapids: Eerdmans, p. 17.
2 Peterson, *Contemplative Pastor*, p. 19.

"who am I going to disappoint today?" Unless I do that, I disappoint people at random, and that's no good.' The point was clear. You can't encourage an unlimited number of people to form unlimited expectations and then try to meet them. For clergy with demanding responsibilities the question is not, 'are you going to disappoint someone today?' It is '*who* are you going to disappoint today?' This suggests an interesting but very real intercession for Morning Prayer. 'Lord, I can't do it all. Please give me your wisdom when it comes to the ministry of disappointing others; and the courage sometimes to disappoint those who will be most cross about it.'

Introducing time wisdom

One of the ways in which people respond to the experience of time poverty is to seek to 'manage' time better. As someone who has a responsibility to help clergy develop in their ministry, I have sought to learn as much as I can about time management and to apply its methods to the reality of ministry. In doing so, I have made a number of observations, which, when taken together, have led me to conclude that although time pressure, time poverty and the experience of busyness leading to frustration and sometimes burnout, are often the *problem*, 'time management' is not the *solution*. That does not mean to say that nothing that goes under the heading 'time management' is of use or relevance, but that the issues are deeper and more sophisticated than we recognize, and that time management is not a weighty or subtle enough tool to address them. Let me briefly set out my observations and then explain more fully the kind of time wisdom that I believe supports all good ministry.

- Time management is based on the misnomer that time can in fact be managed in some way. The more important reality is that time is objective. What we call 'time management' is, in fact, largely self-management, and self-management needs to be informed by multiple forms of wisdom: self-awareness, analysis of context, framing of appropriate expectations and goals and, underlying all this, strong time wisdom.
- People who come into ministry having been in positions where they would have had to manage time effectively find themselves floundering when faced with the curious and fluctuating demands of public ministry.
- Clergy tend to resist the offer of help with time management and find that courses fail to recognize the complexity of the demands and issues they face. Those involved in clergy ministerial development

complain about clergy failing to make time for their time management days. The sad irony in this reinforces my belief that the solution does not quite meet the problem.

- Connected with this is my suspicion that the techniques of time management assume that ministerial life is much more predictable than it is and that the minister has a consistent level of responsibility, authority and control of situations which do not tie up very closely with the reality or experience of ministry today.

- I am convinced that personality is a significant factor in the way in which we relate to time in general but in particular in the way in which people are able to connect with time management techniques. 'Time management' books, courses and resources seem to me to have been designed and prepared *by* organized types *for* organized types. My hunch is that there are plenty of clergy who are just not the sort of person who functions well by writing a list, prioritizing it, making schedules of work and so on.[3] And even if they are, this does not resolve the fundamental issues they face.

So, if 'time management' is not going to deliver the support and change we need, what is 'time wisdom' and why might it be the answer?

In a way, time wisdom is 'time management plus'. It encourages the use of appropriate time management techniques but insists that they are of little use unless deployed alongside a growing awareness of our 'temporal personality' and our appreciation of temporal phenomena. But more than this, time wisdom involves delving into the mystery and spirituality of time itself. By developing time wisdom we become more effective in mission and ministry and more alert and responsible in our stewardship of time. But more significantly, we enter into a deeper relationship with God by engaging in the spirituality of created time and our subjective experience of it.

'Time wisdom', then, is the combination of skills, habits, insights and qualities that lies behind effective use of time by those in ministry who face competing demands, multiple priorities and high expectations from different sources. It is based on awareness of self and others as beings who not only inhabit time but have a temporal dimension to who they are. Time wise people appreciate not only the linear time which is passing away but also the rhythms of life with their complex overlapping and interacting patterns; they have a feel for both the demands of *chronos* and the opportunities of *kairos*. They are attuned to both the objectivity

---

3 Ann McGee-Cooper's *Time Management for Unmanageable People* makes these points and tries to break the mould by offering creative and fun ideas for time management.

and the subjectivity of time and are alert to its physical and spiritual dynamics. They are familiar with 'Parkinson's Law' which says that all work will expand to fill the time available and take responsibility for what one might call the strategic or responsible deployment of time. Time wise people will realize that time is *both* infinite *and* limited and they will quicken their pace, maybe even raise their voice and spring into hasty action when there is a crisis to be dealt with. But a time wise person will also have enough inner conviction and skill in assertion to prevent them becoming victim to cultures or individuals who manipulate things to give the impression that life is one long crisis to be raced through before time runs out. Time wise people will also know that far more can be achieved over the medium to long term provided a process or plan of action is sketched out, engagement with the key issues is on a 'little and often' basis and there is determination and discipline to stay with the task when it is no longer new and is neither exciting nor close to being concluded. Indeed, high-quality time wisdom involves seeing all projects, goals and aspirations both against short-term deadlines and in the context of the broader sweeps of possible time. Persistence is part of the mix.

Developing time wisdom

This sketch of time wisdom, and my assumption that all good ministry is based on a high level of time wisdom, raises the question of how it might be developed. The time wise answer is that it is developed slowly. It is said that Ludwig Wittgenstein suggested that philosophers should always greet each other with the words 'take your time'. What he meant was that the really important things can't be rushed. Serious thought and reflection do not lead to a quick turn around of issues. Another way of putting this would be to suggest that time wisdom is a contemporary way to refer to the virtue of *patience*. It is not what we usually mean by patience – which is the quality which allows us to cope with delay. Time wisdom involves more than accepting that some things take longer than we hoped. It recognizes that if we adjust ourselves well to the contingencies, issues and problems we face, and fit ourselves into the physical and spiritual reality of time, then things start to come together and we overcome our nervous drivenness and self-important busyness. Sometimes this will involve us spending less time on things and getting to the end of the piece of work or ministerial task much more quickly than we had thought. Other times it will involve slowing the pace and taking longer. On yet other occasions we will settle into the reality that what we are engaged in is not 'project-like' at all and that it is part of the open-endedness of the ministry of presence and witness, those vital and vigilant activities which are not about making a difference or being effective but which reflect constancy, steadfastness and faithfulness. Time wise ministers see themselves not as slaves to another demand or early deadline but as the servants of a God whose providence and purpose unfold at uneven and unexpected paces. They understand the importance of seeking to accommodate to this timing rather than impose their own. However, in the contemporary Church, where clergy often carry responsibility for several benefices and where people carry significant diocesan portfolios alongside other demanding roles (area deans are much on my mind as I write this), it is no longer sustainable to engage in public ministry as if it were one long residency. Our mission context demands intentional, focused and strategic activity – in a word, 'projects', and it is when we are engaged with these that the time management ideas can be most helpfully deployed. But it is the interaction and overlap between this and the ministry of presence and availability and the commitment to a spirituality and theology that is so much richer, as well as being more meaningful and hopeful, than the ever faster ticking of the secular clock, which demands this profound quality of time wisdom.

Some resources for developing time wisdom are listed at the end of the chapter. I want to conclude, however, by suggesting that one thing that can be worked at in the early years of ministry (and which needs attention over the years) is the development of what might be called, by analogy with a landscape, a 'timescape'.

Timescape

It is hard for me to imagine a living form of Christianity without some sort of timescape. Time is so vast and disorienting that unless it is broken up a bit, shaped and ordered then we risk getting lost in the chaos of it and being driven along by the urgency of the latest demand. Few people today will be able to fit into an existing timescape but all who face the physical, spiritual and temporal demands of public ministry need to develop a timescape that might sustain them over the longer haul.

A healthy timescape has three qualities. It is in some way derived from and connected to the timescape of the Church. It is realistic about your stage in life and the demands and needs of those who share your life with you. It has a firm but flexible quality so that when for whatever reason you pull it out of shape, it slowly reverts to a healthy and sustainable form.

The Church has been a timescaping institution for many centuries and it is wise to think that maybe it has got a few things right. In particular, its connecting of corporate and Eucharistic worship with the first day of the week and daily prayer with the morning and evening. The point about such disciplines is not that only 100 per cent attainment is good enough. It is that the habit of it begins to calm the chaos and bring a rhythm to life which allows for regular engagement with Scripture, sacrament and prayer. Time for work and leisure needs to be factored into our personal timescape too. Today's Church is more deliberate in declaring the expectation of days worked, though it is not very specific about hours. Some have encouraged an expectation in the newly ordained that they will work two sessions out of three each day of the week and have a clear and regular 'day off'. Few who have been in ministry for a number of years can look back and say that this is the way it has worked out for them and I am not in conscience able to offer this as a recommendation. However, at this point I should come clean and say that I really don't feel that the phrase 'day off' reflects a high level of time wisdom. 'Free day' or 'day for leisure' is more like it. Some speak of the need of a 'coasting' day in addition to a day which is free from objective ministerial demands and so free for other purposes. This might typically be a Saturday when few appointments will be made and there is a different pace of life to a normal ministerial day and yet is not quite 'free'. That sounds like good advice to me. But there is also a need to recognize that ministry is responsive and requires flexibility of us and, like all people with real responsibilities, there will be times when we have to deal with unexpected and priority-changing surprises and whole periods of time which are dominated by crisis. A well-developed timescape will help the minister retain some shape to their life in such times. But it is not right, I believe, to uses one's timescape or 'Rule of Life' as a defence against the demands of a genuine crisis. Jesus' critique of the religiosity of sabbath keeping must ever be on our minds. The point about a well developed timescape is that it is strong enough to be there when we have lost sight of it. A good timescape has a homely and hospitable quality. You might even say that a robust and valuable timescape is a very gracious and forgiving one.

A good timescape will reflect the realities of your life. If you have a young family there is no point in trying to live as if you don't. But equally if you are in public ministry there is no point in pretending to your family that you are not. The reality is that one will inevitably impinge on the other. Your task, as the time wise person at the overlap, is to do what you can to ensure that this intimate connectedness is healthy and life-giving over the long haul. This is an area where we can be sure that we will *not* always get it right, but knowing that might make it easier to make the best of things; and that can be far better than we often hope or imagine. But just as every priest is different, so too is every family and every local church. All these things have to be worked out graciously and patiently as a sustainable timescape is formed.

Another reality to be reflected is stage in ministry. Those who are ordained relatively young, as I was, may possibly need more time for reflection and recovery after difficult pastoral encounters than people with greater life experience. We all vary in terms of how much we take on board of other people's suffering, and how readily we adjust from sad to joyful situations, and it is easy for those who do so readily to be impatient with those who need to reflect and ruminate a bit more. People also vary in the time they need to prepare, especially for liturgical participation and for preaching. In all these areas there is need for both discipline and wisdom. The need for 'recovery' and 'preparation' can sometimes become an excuse to avoid other demands. One of the lessons that clergy in training posts have to learn is how to prepare when there is, it seems, no time to prepare. They also need to find ways to help them adjust from one demanding situation to another when they follow quickly on. I recall the Saturday when as a curate I went straight from a hospital visit with a couple whose baby had died to a wedding. When an incumbent, I conducted a wedding during Princess Diana's funeral, there being far more flowers in the churchyard for the Princess than in the church for the bride. There were strange and difficult dissonances caused precisely by timing on both occasions. Training incumbents also need to appreciate that the skills involved in this can only be acquired slowly, and that very often what happens when more experienced people adjust or prepare quickly is that they are drawing on years of experience, reflection, study and prayer. And sometimes they are not adjusting at all; they are just going from situation to situation without making a deep connection and rather than preparing quickly are failing to prepare at all – just delivering their 'same old, same old'. This is not time wisdom. It is failure to spot how that which was once new and fresh does, alas, become old and stale, simply with the passage of, yes, *time*.

Other aspects of a timescape will emerge in a local context as a particular ministry develops. Extended periods away from duties, such as holidays and retreats and sabbaticals, need to be part of this and like the free day there is value in the anticipation as well as the reality, so they do need to be in the diary, looked forward to and prepared for. Above all the pattern of giving and receiving, exerting and recovering, depleting and renewing, needs to be honoured. If this is done wisely and with generous self-awareness and careful supervision the new minister will develop ministerial stamina. This is a vital consideration. The aim is not only to manage well the demands of this day or week but to form a time-scape that, while it will continue to evolve, will help a minister to give of their best over decades of service.

Concluding remarks

Both time and ministry are deep, complex, mysterious subjects and so it should not be too surprising that there are many issues to be discussed and resolved when they interact and overlap. In this chapter I have tried to explore some of the theology of time and to connect that with the lived experience of ministry today. Good ministry is based not on the application of the principles of 'time management' but on something much richer, theological and nuanced: 'time wisdom'. Time wisdom is informed by many kinds of knowledge and awareness including intuition and emotional intelligence, spirituality and theology. That there is a need for all in ministry to seek to develop time wisdom is evident by the experience of time poverty and the self-presentation of many clergy as 'busy'. Developing time wisdom, however, is not a matter of attending a course or using a resource or method, nor is it likely to be a quick fix. It is a matter of attending to the experience, psychology and spirituality of time and working through trial and error, and with sustained and disciplined reflection, over the years. Time wisdom cannot be boiled down to a short list of key points. But maybe one question needs to be given a hearing more regularly than we often allow. It is this: 'how wise am I being with regard to time?' Offer that question to God in patience and hope and see what comes back by way of answer.

Resources to help develop time wisdom

S. Cherry, 2012, *Beyond Busyness: Time Wisdom for Ministry*, Durham: Sacristy Press.

J. K. Clemens and S. Dalrymple, 2005, *Time Mastery*, London: Amacom.

Ann McGee-Cooper, 1993, *Time Management for Unmanageable People*, New York: Bantam.

Eugene Peterson, 1998, *The Contemplative Pastor*, Grand Rapids: Eerdmans.

Philip Zimbardo and Philip Boyd, 2008, *The Time Paradox*, New York: Rider.

8

Enabling Ministry

LESLEY BENTLEY

How often do we hear the phrase, 'Going to church?' or 'Are you a churchgoer?' Fixed in the English psyche and even in the psyche of many worshipping Christians is the notion that church is something we go to. The understanding may encompass a group of people, not just a building, but is nevertheless something one attends. It follows easily from this that the vicar is the chaplain of that group of people, the one who makes things happen, most commonly worship, that people can go to. From this it follows just as easily that those who are the activists in church life are there to help the vicar.

In this chapter, I set out to explore how this view of the Church can be turned on its head. Indeed, that the incumbent or any other ordained minister is there to enable the Church to be the Church, to enable God's people to grow as disciples, to grow in community and to engage in the ministry to which they have been called through their baptism and in which they continue to be called as disciples. The view is put forward, from experience of incumbency and the training of other clergy, that the ministry of incumbents can be described in seven words, expressed in three phrases. This may seem rather a bold assertion, given the hours many incumbents, in many dioceses, have spent on their role descriptions, following the introduction of Common Tenure. Here are the seven words in their three dimensions: model discipleship, enable ministry and hold the vision. The assistant minister, priest or deacon assists in this work.

At the end of the section on each of the dimensions there are suggestions drawn from my parochial ministry about how these dimensions might be developed.

Model discipleship

At the heart of our faith is our calling as disciples of Jesus Christ. Jesus calls people in the Gospels first to follow, Matthew 4.19, 'Come, follow me, and I will make you fishers of men' (NIV), before he commissions them to

work (Matt. 28.19). He takes the disciples through a time of formation
as they minister with him, at times learning the greatness of their calling
and the way in which the Holy Spirit would work in them and through
them. (In Luke 9.2 Jesus sends the Twelve out. They report back all they
have done in verse 10.) At times they have to learn from their mistakes
(Matt. 17.14–21, a failed attempt at healing). Our first calling is as disciples. *Shaping the Future*, the Ministry Division document of 2006, describes
discipleship as 'the whole-life response of Christians to Jesus Christ. Everything a Christian believes and does is potentially an aspect of discipleship:
the goal of discipleship is to grow ever more Christ-like in every aspect of
life.'[1] The report recognizes that '[t]he primary focus of discipleship is the
service of God and His mission in the world' and that 'many lay people see
such service as their vocation and ministry'.[2] It is this understanding of the
term ministry, that encompasses all service of God and neighbour, that I
will be using in this chapter rather than that used in the report which refers
to publicly authorized ministry. Publicly authorized ministry is thus one
form of the ministry that discipleship encompasses.

Discipleship is about the whole of our lives. This includes not just the way
we behave, the way we steward our personal resources and the way we relate to others, it includes our willingness to share the gospel and to minister
to others, wherever we are. Being outside the parish for clergy may mean
time to be more relaxed, but not time to relax our calling. This theme of our
continuing discipleship and development in the ways of Christ is dealt with
in more depth in Andrew Mayes' chapter in this book.

The *Common Worship* ordinal asks this question about discipleship:
'Will you endeavour to fashion your own life and that of your household
according to the way of Christ, that you may be a pattern and example to
God's people?'

Living in a vicarage is often described as like living in a goldfish bowl.
One former incumbent writes about a parish:

> I at once applauded and resented the voluntary churchyard maintenance
> team who began work on the dot of 9.00am on a Saturday, through spring,
> summer and autumn. I delighted in the work they did, the wonderful ap-
> pearance of our graveyard and the fact that they did not start before I was
> ready to get up out of bed. I resented their knowing, not that Saturday was
> my usual day off, but what time I usually got up on my day off.

---

1 Ministry Division of the Archbishops' Council, 2005, *Shaping the Future: New Patterns of
Training for Lay and Ordained*, London: Church House Publishing, p. 4.
2 Ibid.

We are called not just to be disciples but to model discipleship, and we will get plenty of opportunity, because in parish ministry we are so visible. This is, of course, not easy for our families (for those of us who have families living with them) on whom there is often a similar expectation, although not without some scriptural warrant (1 Tim. 3.12b).

In modelling discipleship and the attempt to grow in discipleship, we will also aim to encourage this in others. The very act of modelling does that. We will also be able to encourage from the pulpit and in other areas of leadership, with an integrity that makes this real. I offer a few suggestions based upon my own ministry about how we can make this happen.

- Help the congregation to understand the story of its members. A friend used Lent to encourage congregational members from hugely different social and life backgrounds to tell their stories and the stories of their walk with God. Often all the congregation know of each other is what they see in corporate worship or within other church settings. These stories helped others to understand the exercise of faith outside of the church, within the family or work context. The congregation was not only inspired through the stories but members were better able to understand themselves. Often people see only a part of what the church community is doing. Small groups can also help Christians to share their lives albeit with a limited number of people.
- Encourage members of the congregation and invited guests to talk about work outside the church that is consistent with kingdom values. A wider involvement in the community is clearly of missional value of itself. The chance to 'make a difference' will energize members of the congregation and also enable those in the community to see Christian values being lived out. This then becomes a powerful evangelistic tool.
- Support new Christians in telling others about their new experience of faith. Like the woman at the well (John 4), they are often good evangelists. An account of a new-found experience, however inarticulate, is often very powerful.

Enable ministry

In the introduction to the *Common Worship* service for the ordination of priests, the Bishop reads a description of priestly ordination:

God calls his people to follow Christ, and forms us into a royal priest-hood, a holy nation, to declare the wonderful deeds of him who has called us out of darkness into his marvellous light.

The Church is the body of Christ, the people of God and the dwelling place of the Holy Spirit. In baptism the whole Church is summoned to witness to God's love and to work for the coming of his kingdom.

To serve this royal priesthood, God has given particular ministries. Priests are ordained to lead God's people in the offering of praise and the proclamation of the gospel.

The calling to encourage discipleship within the Church will naturally lead to service of God and neighbour in ministry. A description follows in the ordinal of the work of the priest:

> they are to sustain the community of the faithful by the ministry of word and sacrament, that we all may grow into the fullness of Christ and be a living sacrifice acceptable to God.

Corporate worship will be a key part of the nurture of discipleship and ministry. The representative role of the priest within worship draws the Christian community together before God, in self-offering and the com-munal reception of his Holy Spirit. The calling of all the baptized to min-istry is a part of the calling to discipleship. It is the working out of that discipleship in the Church and in the world. That all may be 'living sacri-fices' picks up the writing of Paul in Romans 12.1, 'Therefore, I urge you, brothers [sic], in view of God's mercy, to offer your bodies as living sac-rifices, holy and pleasing to God – which is your spiritual act of worship' (NIV). The chapter goes on to describe the familiar image of the body and the different functions of all members (12.4). 'We have different gifts, ac-cording to the grace given us' (12.6, NIV).

If the priest is to serve this royal priesthood then a function of his or her role, in leading God's people in praise and proclamation, will be in enabling each member (to use Paul's term) to develop gifts and to harness skills and experience already gained for the ministry of each of the baptized. This is reflected in the ordinal in the introduction to the declarations:

> Guided by the Spirit, they are to discern and foster the gifts of all God's people, that the whole Church may be built up in unity and faith.

The ordinal uses a number of phrases that emphasize the communal nature of the Church: 'the body of Christ', a 'royal priesthood', a 'holy nation'.

In a recent paper Stephen Pickard draws attention to the many ways in which the Church is distracted from this unity, as he describes 'key moves'[3] that are required 'in order for the Church's ministry to remain firmly Christian and properly Catholic'. The strength of the paper is in its focus which goes beyond the identification of the split between clergy and laity to tensions arising from the societal context in which the Church of England finds itself. He describes a need to move from fragmentation to integration, from mechanistic to organic theory and practice, from competition to co-operation, from skills to character, and from structure to energy.

Within the context of describing the key move required from fragmentation to integration, Pickard describes from an historical viewpoint the 'longstanding split between clergy and laity' which he traces back to Clement of Rome, writing at the end of the first century.[4] He describes this split as supported in the present by the 'western preoccupation with the individual and more recent emphasis upon professionalism, performance and success'.[5] As Pickard notes, Robin Greenwood's work is one of a number that seek to 'develop more integrative accounts of the ministries of the Church'.[6] In *Parish Priests: For the Sake of the Kingdom*, he pays tribute to the work of Schillebeeckx and others in 'showing how no authentic ministry stands apart from a particular church community'.[7] Greenwood develops his understanding of *koinonia* in relation to an understanding of the Church and the existence of ordained and lay, together in ministry. 'A koinonia ecclesiology makes room for the separate and distinct orders of ministry to be in creative and dynamic relationship.'[8] 'The parish priest has no existence except in relation with fellow members of the baptized community.'[9] 'It is the entire church that enacts the *episcope* that releases God's love within the whole church, for the fulfilment of creation.'[10] This rather goes beyond the wording of the ordinal, 'They [priests] share with the Bishop in the oversight of the Church, delighting in its beauty and rejoicing in its well-being.'

---

3 S. Pickard, 2011, 'A Christian Future for the Church's Ministry: Some Critical Moves', p. 1. A revised and expanded version (privately circulated) of S. Pickard, 2010, 'The Collaborative Character of Christian Ministry', *Expository Times*, June 2010.

4 Pickard, 2011, p. 2.

5 Pickard, 2011, p. 5.

6 Robin Greenwood, 1994, *Transforming Priesthood*, London: SPCK.

7 Robin Greenwood, 2009, *Parish Priests: For the Sake of the Kingdom*, London: SPCK. p. xiv.

8 Greenwood, 2009, p. 22.

9 Greenwood, 2009, p. 100.

10 Greenwood, 2009, p. xii.

There are a variety of ways of helping people to develop their gifts and to use their skills and experience within the life of the Church. Training and mentoring gives confidence as well as knowledge and ability. A culture of acceptance of mistakes and failure as others move forward will aid this.

It is perhaps harder to enable people to develop a ministry outside the Church, perhaps in the workplace or local community. The Church as a whole is particularly poor at this in relation to the recognition and understanding of ministry in the workplace. Initial steps can be made by valuing ministry outside the Church within the preaching and teaching of the Church, as mentioned in the suggestions above. Small groups can be a place for confidential sharing of a ministry.

I offer some suggestions from my parochial ministry to assist in enabling ministry within the church community.

- Actively seek out people for new ministries. This may at first seem possible only within congregations of the professional and articulate, but this is not necessarily the case. David, an older man, who used to be active in the church but was no longer so, was surprised by being asked to join a teenage confirmation class as another adult presence. He really enjoyed the opportunity to relate to another age group and soon took up other areas of ministry within the church. Experience within diocesan local ministry schemes is of many people taking small steps towards public ministry with the affirmation of other participants and their parishes.
- Always listen seriously to offers of people to engage in ministry. 'We feel a call to do something about the housing estate that we can see from the upstairs windows of our new house' was the beginning in my last parish of a Fresh Expression within a pub in the parish. Those who had approached me were new members of the church, they sought the backing of the PCC and drew together a small group who, despite their activist natures, spent many months listening and praying before their first 'event' and many more months before establishing regular gatherings.
- Develop a culture of letting people resign a ministry if they make this choice. People find it harder to begin if they think they will 'end up doing it forever'. They find it harder to test out an area of ministry if they think that they will not be allowed to let go if they discern that it is not for them.
- Create a climate where the gift of newness is valued. Too often churches expect new members to 'learn how we do things'. A new member joining a congregation explained that he and his family had

been worshipping for some months with a neighbouring congregation. 'They were lovely people, very welcoming, but eventually we realized that they just wanted us to fit in, to be one of them. They were not interested in anything new we had to offer.' Over the years he developed his ministry and followed a vocation to ordination. This blocking attitude is often hidden in the phrase, 'they need to get to know how we do things here'.

Hold the vision

The only question in the ordinal that relates directly to the people of God is 'Will you lead Christ's people in proclaiming his glorious gospel, so that the good news of salvation may be heard in every place?' Proclamation of the kingdom is at the heart of the Great Commission of Matthew 28 and so at the heart of the work to which we are called, the work of ministry, whether this proclamation is through word or deed. Jesus' manifesto is declared in Luke 4.18–19 where he is clear that his mission is to the poor and the outcast. It is his work in which we are called to join and it is clear that mission and outreach are at its heart. However we describe the vision of our local churches, it is God's work in which we join and it is clear that mission must be a key and integral part. The ultimate vision is God's, not ours.

If it is God's vision in which we are called to share, then we need to take care in the discernment of that vision. This is not a task for the ordained ministers alone, or for a small in-group, but for the whole people of God. Clearly the first step in the discernment is prayer but it may also be necessary for there to be teaching concerning the values of the kingdom before such discernment can become a possibility. In any case, clear communication about the task and its importance will need to take place. A number of techniques for discernment of the vision may be used, for example congregational meetings, away days, surveys, small group discussions. Tools for wider church reflection such as *The Healthy Churches' Handbook*[11] or the Natural Church Development surveys[12] will stimulate thinking. Putting the vision into action will mean, at times, making hard choices. Sometimes this can be between two good possibilities, where one must take priority in fulfilment of the vision because this is all that can be currently resourced.

---

11 R. Warren, 2004, *The Healthy Churches' Handbook*, London: Church House Publishing.
12 www.ncd-uk.com.

As incumbents or assistant priests or deacons we are called to guard that vision, to enable the church to focus on that rather than the everyday minutiae of buildings, tea and coffee rotas, and fundraising events. A focus on mission is often hard to hold, particularly where a church has become a place of refuge for the few. Mission means going out beyond the refuge and the possibility of change within it. If we can maintain a focus on an outward-looking vision, then as churches we will be considerably helped in our setting of priorities among our activities. Below I have suggested a couple of ways that we can encourage this in parish ministry.

- Set goals that those who are involved on the ground in ministry can relate to. A couple of years into my last incumbency I arranged a PCC awayday to set aims and objectives for the next year. I made the arrangements at a well-attended PCC, and everyone could come. When the day came, all the directly elected PCC members had sent their apologies. I realized that, although the aim of the meeting was good, it was the wrong place to fulfil that aim. It was clearly not a priority for PCC members. On the other hand, when I gathered together the leaders of different areas of ministry the following year and asked them to define aims, there was an excitement and a clear picture. The PCC then took on a governance role, looking at the big picture, defined by the vision statement that had been put together corporately, and identifying areas that needed encouragement.
- Encourage the congregation to tell its story. In one congregation I learnt of a great deal of financial sacrifice made, in the face of what was perceived as opposition from the diocese, around 50 years ago. This had enabled the congregation and the church building to survive, was an inspiration in the present but also explained some unexpected attitudes to change in the building.

Drawing the strands together

These elements – modelling discipleship, enabling ministry, and holding the vision – can only function if drawn together as a whole. One of the toughest steps in ordained ministry is the move from curacy to incumbency. The incumbent's role, often now described as an episcopal role, is to hold all the strands together through a ministry of oversight. The assistant minister supports this and, in doing this, may carry much responsibility.

Some widely used images helped me to understand this as I developed in my ministry as an incumbent. When I began ministry in my last parish,

I was asked by my mentor to describe my image of the parish. The image that came to mind was that of a large ocean liner. The ship was running smoothly, with a well-organized crew, but going nowhere. It was tied up at the quay. A lot of people were involved in running the church, the activities of the congregation and some outreach, but there was no overall sense of direction. In other words, people were behaving as faithful disciples, many were engaged in service of others within church, community and secular organizations, but a sense of direction or vision was lacking. My mentor shared his image of a previous parish where he had been vicar, as that of a helicopter. He must have imagined himself as the engine, because he described it as requiring a lot of work to keep it going. Referring back to the seven words above, my parish had enabled ministry, but was weak on vision. His parish had less of either. My thoughts moved to an image of how I would like things to be. I chose the orchestra because within this image each person exercised their role. Some were more active than others; some more capable than others, but all were moving together towards a common goal, under the direction of the conductor, the playing of a beautiful piece of music. I found this model helpful for a long time. The role of the conductor allowed me to enable ministry and hold the vision, as I continued in my discipleship and calling.

As ministry grew in the parish I realized that the model remained inadequate. Someone suggested to me the model of a jazz group. The group works together, within a shared piece of music. The leader is much less obvious, because they are playing their own instrument within the group. There is a common framework within the piece of music, but each musician is able to improvise around the theme, but only in a way that is complementary to the other instruments. There is room for innovation. The unexpected is possible. Presumably some mistakes occur, but if the remainder of the group is working well, they will somehow be incorporated so that the piece of music continues. The model is a clearer one for the outworking of the seven words. It enables the vision to be held, but allows flexibility in the way it is worked through. There is a role for the leader, but not as one who controls in either a dominating way or a more subtle way. Others are empowered in a way that the leader may not have dreamed. The leader 'presides' but in a way that enables others to develop, so that the leadership is one of service. He or she is part of the whole, but with a distinctive role. Looking to the needs of the other and supporting them are also drawn out in this model. As you may have guessed, I was working in a largish suburban parish. But the model has a wider application than just that type of church. The jazz ensemble is usually small. This does not mean that people cannot innovate or find new ways of working together.

The role of episcope, working in the power of the Spirit to enable the Church to function together as a whole, is not one that can easily be undertaken during curacy. One approach to curacy is to define it by pastoral tasks, particularly if that curacy is short in duration, or split across a deanery and the work of several incumbents. A misuse of the House of Bishops' Learning Outcomes can lead to a ministry that is focused around success in projects or areas designed to meet a series of outcomes, rather than one that is embedded in a local community or communities, supporting and enabling the local church to be the body of Christ in that area. If curacy is to lead to a ministry that enables the whole Church, where clergy and lay work alongside each other for the good of the kingdom of God, then the focus needs to be on the big picture, the picture of God's people engaged in worship, ministry and outreach in a local area. Greenwood writes that 'parish priests (within teams of many kinds) should not regard as their primary role the provision of ministry to others. Rather, precisely thorough the celebration of the sacraments, preaching and pastoral care they are to stimulate, interweave and support God's calling of us all.'[13] Time spent by a training incumbent in regular supervision and reflection and enabling the curate to understand the whole picture of their ministry, including that which they as curates will not be a part of, such as the constant calls to the Vicarage or difficult discussions with individual PCC members, will be invaluable in enabling the curate to understand and reflect upon the work of episcope within the parish. There is sometimes a tendency, on the part of training ministers, to protect the curate from what may feel like 'management' and allow them instead to engage all the time in the practicalities of ministry. This leaves the curate exposed and inexperienced when faced with an incumbency or even, in the case of a permanent assistant priest, an interregnum or the illness of the incumbent. This need not be the case.

Many, if not most, of the readers of this chapter will be working in situations with a number of churches or parishes. If priestly ministry is defined by pastoral tasks we are bound to frustration. It is impossible for one priest to fulfil all that is commonly expected of the Church of England in that parish. Pastoral care and presence are at the core of Christian ministry, but this is the ministry of the whole Church, not one person or a small group of people. I have watched in the village where I live, where the local church is part of a team of ten churches with two full-time clergy, the local people take more and more responsibility for the local church. It was the churchwarden who approached me last year to lead a memorial service, a new initiative that was part of their local mission action plan.

---

13 Greenwood, *Parish Priests*, p. xii.

The words with which we began – model discipleship, enable ministry and guard the vision – are not words that describe a list of tasks. They describe the 'how' of ministry rather than the 'what'. They describe something that is less tangible than 'take a funeral' and 'lead worship', but nevertheless key to sustainable ministry in any situation. They describe a ministry that is shared by the whole community of the Church.

The collect in the ordination services makes clear the joining of all faithful people, disciples of Christ, in ministry. This chapter concludes with that prayer:

God our Father,
Lord of all the world,
Through your Son you have called us into the fellowship
Of your universal Church:
Hear our prayer for your faithful people
that in their vocation and ministry
each may be an instrument of your love,
and give to your servant now to be ordained
the needful gifts of grace.

9

Preaching for Today

SIMON BAKER

In this chapter I will consider some things which I think are key to the call to preach among God's people in the twenty-first century. In doing this I shall draw upon some ideas and authors that have influenced me and the way I approach the task and privilege of preaching. I believe that the most important thing is for each preacher to find their own authentic voice. The ideas and writings of others can contribute to this but in the end the preacher's person, their faith and their preaching all have to have integrity. This does not mean that the preacher's voice cannot change or that it has to be just one voice. Part of the challenge of preaching is to try out different voices and see if they can become your own. The changing circumstances and experience of ministry mean that the preacher's voice will adapt and evolve. For me the most exciting thing about preaching over the last 30 years has been the growing confidence to preach not as I think other people would expect but as I believe the Holy Spirit is calling me.

To be open to the prompting of the Holy Spirit means being attentive not only to the Spirit in prayer, but also to the word of God in Scripture and the life of the community.

Preaching is part of a dialogue and the preacher is engaged in a many-voiced conversation with a community of people who have heard Christ's call to follow him. Hearing the call to follow leads to expectation that there is a next step to take, and then another, in the journey of faith. This journey and these steps are not taken alone but in community and the preacher has the task of pointing the way and nourishing people for the journey.

> Preaching . . . is a monologue, in that one person undertakes an extended speech, but provisional, rather than final, in that it stems from listening and invites further speech in turn. Preaching, that is, is neither a single word nor the final word; rather it exists to prompt and nurture the larger conversation of the faithful.[1]

---

1 David J. Lose, 2003, *Confessing Jesus Christ: Preaching in a Postmodern World*, Grand Rapids: Eerdmans, p. 107.

The intention of the sermon is both pastoral and missional. It is pastoral in that the preacher has a care for the people who are addressed; they are God's people in that place, loved and precious in his sight. Their concerns, their joys, their fears, their hopes, their questions, their interests all form the context for the preacher and into this the preacher is charged to speak with awareness and understanding. Preaching is missional, because it is intended to grow the discipleship of those gathered together and open the way for others to become disciples.

Because preaching is set in the context of worship, when God's people are gathered, it is an activity that is particular and related to certain times and places. In other words preaching is 'occasional'. As a word in an ongoing conversation around holiness and discipleship in the world, the sermon is something that is only for that moment in the dialogue. The sermon must be appropriate for this point in the conversation of faith among these people.

James Nieman claims that the preacher must pay careful attention to context because the sermon is a *timely* word.

> Paradoxically, although preachers utter something treasured as worthwhile for all generations, they can only do so within their own generation. This is actually a liberating realization, for we need not 'say it all' in a timelessly true yet assuredly remote sermon, but simply the word that is enough for today.[2]

One key question that every preacher must ask is, 'What makes this a word from God for these people in this place on this day?' Though the preacher may find that ideas, images and insights can be re-used and refreshed in future preaching the preacher should be wary of ever re-preaching that particular sermon without asking this key question. The moment in the life of the community, the life of the world, and indeed the life of the preacher which made this sermon the word of God for now, will never come again.

Preaching brings the story of God into the lives and story of both individuals and community. In doing this it intends to transform and change. Preaching does this by bringing Scripture and contemporary life into conversation with one another to create an encounter with the living God. As Nieman says:

> Preaching is not really about bridging from an ancient and arcane scriptural world into a current and complex social reality, so that knowing

---

2 J. R. Nieman, 2008, *Knowing the Context*, Minneapolis: Fortress Press, p. 9.

more about each end of that bridge produces more effective communication . . . Instead, preaching bears a living encounter between the God we know chiefly through Jesus and a contemporary people that trusts this God as the source of their life. This encounter happens not as a mental idea or a vague force but through direct divine participation in actual human reality. God risked identifying with Israel, both its glories and its shame. Jesus touched diseased bodies, accepting their wounds as his own. The Spirit visited fearful disciples driving them beyond closed doors. Preaching represents just this kind of encounter with all who will listen, an embodied way God enters into our lives.[3]

Because preaching is part of a conversation the preacher is called not so much to preach *to* people or *at* them but to preach the gospel *with* them, *through* this particular moment and the possibilities for grace that it offers.

What David Schlafer says about preaching on special occasions is applicable to all preaching.

We have to help people see *how*, not simply inform them *that*, God is present here and now. Helping listeners grasp how God's love is distinctly manifest through the life of a saint, in the midst of troubled disagreement, in the silence shaped by a retreat meditation, in the tragic conditions of a death, in the joyful occasion of a wedding, in the unlikely event of a secular holiday – that is the goal towards which the special occasion sermon needs to strive . . . The ultimate impact of such preaching will extend far beyond the setting of the particular occasional sermon. If those who hear a sermon can see how God is present to them, perhaps unexpectedly, through *this* time and place their imaginations will be stretched and sparked to see for themselves the constant grace of God in other times and places as well.[4]

If the preacher is to preach through the occasion they must engage with both the Scriptures and the context of the community into which they will speak. The Scriptures lay before us how God has called people and how people have responded to that call. The present context of the community gathered together is the moment of God's call *now* and the moment of response *now*.

3 Nieman, *Knowing the Context*, p. 6.
4 David Schlafer, 1998, *What Makes This Day Different: Preaching Grace on Special Occasions*, New York: Cowley, p. 18.

The cultural context in which preaching sits has changed radically, at least in the Church in the West, and this affects the way in which the preacher approaches the task of preaching and the way in which others hear and receive what is preached. In our postmodern context (however difficult to define) it is clear that figures and words of authority are not received in the way they once were. Further, the Scriptures themselves, once regarded as determinative text for individuals and communities, are not now seen by most people as a primary reference for personal morality and lifestyle or for guidance in organizing affairs or institutions. To illustrate this we can look briefly at two passages which might stand as metaphors for how things perhaps once were and hold them up as a contrast to help us reflect upon how things are today.

Case study

2 Samuel 12.1–7a

Nathan appears before David to pronounce the Lord's judgement on him for the death of Uriah the Hittite and the taking of Bathsheba.

- Nathan has the right and duty to appear before the King who must hear his words.
- It is part of the 'covenant' between the King and God.
- Nathan's story, David's response and God's judgement 'describe reality'.

The role of Nathan as speaker for God is not marginalized but is at the very centre of the political and religious establishment. He and what he does are part of what it means for David to be king, though it is uncomfortable.

Nathan does not seek to radically challenge kingly rule but rather to critique the practices of a king who is God's anointed.

The Church in Christendom might have been in that kind of place but is not so now. What the Church and the individual preacher say about God and the gospel is not part of the accepted range of descriptions of how things are.

Think about

How have you addressed political or social justice issues in your preaching? How did people respond?

2 Chronicles 34.14–33

Hilkiah the priest finds the book of the law in the house of the Lord.

- It is recognized as 'holy' – the word of God.
- Josiah, the King, the priests and the people accept the book as true description of reality.
- It is received as setting out how things should be, in contrast to the ways of the ancestors.

In our contemporary context the Bible is not the dominant text. It is not accepted by all as the primary description of reality or as determinative of how society or individuals should live.

Think about

How do you think the response to the authority of Scripture has changed within the Church and the wider community?

Preaching voices

Walter Brueggemann claims that the Scriptures are *now* alternative text and description of reality in contrast to the dominant text and reading of reality in contemporary western society.

> The Biblical text in all its odd disjunctions, is an offer of an alternative script, and preaching this text is an exploration of how the world is if it is imagined through this alternative script. This thesis reminds us of two important recognitions. First the biblical text is indeed a profound alternative to the text of the Enlightenment and therefore alternative to the dominant text with which most of us came to church . . . The second notion here is that the preacher, from this text, does not describe a gospel governed world but helps the congregation imagine it.[5]

Brueggemann draws out what he sees as the stark distinction in values and focus between the Enlightenment, dominant, description of reality and the alternative reality, the way the world might be, which is offered through the subversive text of Scripture.

---

5 Walter Brueggemann, 2007, *The Word Militant*, Minneapolis: Fortress, p. 26.

Whereas the dominant text finds human initiative at the core of reality, the gospel witnesses to holiness as the core, and whereas it is the self that arises out of the hegemonic text, in the gospel it is the neighbor.[6]

Brueggemann recognizes that there is a constant conflict between two 'realities'; the present dominant description of how the world is, and the alternative description of reality seen through Scripture. As Christians we are part of the culture around us, we participate in it and are even dependent upon it. However, we are constantly drawn to see the world and ourselves differently in the light of our primary relationship with God.

Changing times and the tension between culture and gospel lead many to feel that being a Christian in our contemporary society is to be something of a resident alien.

This sense of being alien to the dominant culture offers the possibility of looking at some particular tasks that lie before the preacher. These can be approached as different 'voices' with which the preacher can speak into the conversation in the community.

Mourning for the past

Preachers need to recognize the mourning and bereavement that the community feels for the way things were. The past is gone and is not coming back. For many in the Church it is proving hard to let go of this past.

If the past is gone and we have lost much of what we held dear are we to abandon what we still have in despair? It is hard to sing the Lord's song in a strange land. It may ring hollow or it may stand out starkly and embarrassingly against the prevailing culture.

Mourning for the past is always in danger of falling into nostalgia. *Lamentation* is a key element in contemporary preaching in a time of change. Lamentation is not self-pity or nostalgia but a clear-eyed realization of the tragedy and truths of the past and the present. It focuses upon sinfulness and calls for repentance and renewal.

The preacher has the pastoral task of helping mourners take leave of the past and look to a new future.

Hope for the future

Critical assessment of who we are and what we are about could become corrosive and destructive if it were not for hope. Christian hope does not

---

6 Ibid.

rest on the resources we have to deploy or a place in society to be regained but upon God. Our hope for any kind of future must be a hope in something beyond the present circumstances. Transformation comes from outside. The kingdom of God is not about the re-establishment of how things once were but about bringing in something new.

Christian communities need to practise and cultivate hope: a constant and positive practice of hope in God. The preacher, despite feeling that the Church and the world have changed and things are not what they were, must constantly speak with hope.

Preacher may very properly echo the words of Isaiah as they speak to a community in a time of transition and change, but with hope in the God who will create something new:

> ³ A voice cries out:
> 'In the wilderness prepare the way of the LORD,
>   make straight in the desert a highway for our God.
> ⁴ Every valley shall be lifted up,
>   and every mountain and hill be made low;
> the uneven ground shall become level,
>   and the rough places a plain.
> ⁵ Then the glory of the LORD shall be revealed,
>   and all people shall see it together,
>   for the mouth of the LORD has spoken.'
>
> Isaiah 40.3–5

Memory and identity

In the face of a loss of status and an increasingly pluralistic society there is a great need to establish in the minds of the faith community their common memory and the nature of their identity.

It is hard for people today to belong to, and declare that they belong to, a distinctive community that sees the world radically differently and engages in this with passion.

The stumbling block may be that while many are comfortable to 'belong', they are less comfortable with 'believing' and the demands that both may make upon their lifestyle and choices.

The preacher needs to be a constant teller of the story; the story of salvation; the story of that faith community; the story of individuals who have struggled and found integrity and identity in their relationship with God.

Testimony or *confession* are therefore important 'voices' in contemporary preaching to an alienated community. This means that the preacher must be prepared to share something of themselves and show how their hope in God makes a difference to their own life.

> In short, *I propose that preaching that seeks to be both faithful to the Christian tradition and responsive to our pluralistic, postmodern context is best understood as the public practice of confessing faith in Jesus Christ* . . . By describing such preaching as 'confessional', I seek to reclaim a Christian practice that rests not on empirical proof but on a living confession of faith, leads not to certainty but conviction, and lives not in the domain of knowledge and proof but rather in the realm of faithful assertion.[7]

Anamnesis

Literally this means 'un-forgetting'. Jesus, at the Last Supper, says that breaking bread is a way of un-forgetting him – every time we do this simple and everyday thing. The implication is that a community that starts with a godly passion always forgets, sets its own agenda, offers its own priorities and defends its own concerns. A community that is true to a God who calls needs constantly to un-forget the things that have obscured or veiled the essential truths of its calling.

Breaking open the word of God in Scripture through preaching is a vital way of un-forgetting. In the busyness of life and in the midst of all the tensions and difficulties that people face in the world at large and in the community of the Church it is easy to forget the love, mercy and grace of God. Whether in great set-piece sermons or in short intimate homilies the preacher is called upon to help us 'un-forget' the one thing that most people find it hardest to believe – that God loves them.

Prophecy

The preacher is called to offer subversive, imaginative alternatives that ring true to what we understand of God and his call to be his people. This will lead the preacher to be prophetic both to the community of faith and the wider community in which it is set.

Shaping a vision for the future involves a critique of what is seen and known of the present. But I would suggest that prophecy should not be characterized by the level of indignation, anger or condemnation of

---

7 Lose, *Confessing*, p. 3.

'others' or 'society' that often seems to be the case. This is the kind of prophecy which people often seem to hanker for when they complain that the Church is not prophetic any more. It sets up 'them' and 'us' and establishes 'us' as those who are right.

Rather I suggest, prophecy lies in sowing the seeds of discontent with the way things are and offering the possibility of something new. Prophecy is therefore something for the community itself as well as for those beyond. It is something that is not just for particular moments of criticism and challenge but a constant warning and encouraging voice.

Imagination

Imagination is an important key to how we approach Scripture and how we respond to it. This involves the imagination of the preacher and the imagination of those who hear and apply what they hear to their own lives.

There are a number of 'imaginations' at play here:

- the imagination of the writers/editors of the text(s) of Scripture – what they intend to say or do to their hearer or reader;
- the imagination of the preacher in bringing themselves to the text and the situation they address – their desire to preach *through* both;
- the imagination of the hearers – what they bring to act of hearing on a particular occasion, from knowledge, experience and feelings.

In contrast to the possibilities of imaginative engagement with Scripture there has been, for a long time, the notion that Scripture is a kind of inert container of truths, theological truths. These truths are there for the preacher to discover but only if he or she uses the right tools and approaches the process in a suitably 'clean' and surgical manner.

> So, the preacher's job simply put was to crack the seal, reach inside the textual vessel, draw out the ideas, (thus, *exegesis*), and then produce a sermon somehow applying these ideas to the contemporary situation.[8]

Preachers do not draw pure biblical ideas from texts and then figure out what they might mean for today. In the act of interpretation

---

8 Thomas G. Long, 2005, 'The Use of Scripture in Contemporary Preaching', in D. Day, J. Astley and L. Francis, *A Reader on Preaching*, Aldershot: Ashgate, p. 34.

everything that we know and experience about our present world and everything that we know and experience about the ancient text come together in a volatile, exciting and free ranging moment of imaginative encounter . . . The boldest way to put this is that a certain kind of *eisegesis*, the kind that renders us completely present before the text and passionately concerned to hear a Word that addresses our world, is not a sin to be avoided, but rather an earnestly sought prerequisite to productive *exegesis*.[9]

As different preachers bring themselves and their situation to the text(s), different sermons will be formed and preached. The same Scripture readings will support the breaking open of God's word in a huge variety of ways. The majority of these will be legitimate and faithful at the same time. They are not mutually exclusive.

I believe that it is important to see that the intention of the author does not entirely define or limit what the text might convey. In this way, the work of the preacher in relation to Scripture is free to be influenced by imagination as to how this text might speak to contemporary needs as well as being properly rooted in a respect for the intention and chosen style of the author.

Mark Allen Powell in his book *What Do They Hear? Bridging the Gap between Pulpit and Pew* offers an interesting analysis of the different ways in which preachers and members of congregations hear Scripture and respond to it. He claims that the tendency of the congregational hearer of Scripture texts is to react and respond. They usually stay with the questions, the incongruities, the oddities, the surface. The tendency of the preacher, on the other hand, is to understand and master. They usually move quickly beyond reaction and response to find the 'meaning'.

Most seminaries train their pastors in disciplines of historical criticism (e.g., source criticism, form criticism, and especially redaction criticism) all of which are oriented toward the goal of determining the authorial intention behind ancient texts . . . they are designed to enable the interpreter to understand the text from the perspective of its author, which (for better or worse) is not the perspective from which many of our parishioners engage texts when they find meaning that affects or impacts our lives. Disciplines of literary criticism (e.g., narrative criticism,

9 Long, 'The Use of Scripture', p. 39.

reader-response criticism, and postmodern criticism) tend to assume more of a reader-oriented hermeneutic that can get at what historical critical methods fail to discern.[10]

Powell is not suggesting that more reader-oriented methods should supersede those that look carefully at the author, their context and their intention. Rather, he claims that in the task of preaching the response of the congregation to the word of God read in Scripture needs to be valued and worked with. Perhaps at the heart of this is the distinction that many preachers recognize between a sermon that people find interesting and a sermon that moves them.

Following from this are two key challenges for the congregation and the preacher.

The first challenge is to create an environment in which Scripture is heard with attention and expectation. This will not happen if the readings are poorly delivered but it is completely undermined if people believe (even unconsciously) that their response to God's word does not matter – after all the sermon will come soon and then they will be told the 'meaning'. If the preacher cannot enter with others into the journey of hearing and responding then they will miss a vital point of connection with the congregation.

The second challenge is to remain (at least for a time) with the questions, the puzzlement, the incongruities, the oddities, the excitement, even the scandal that the passage presents. This is important because, if Powell is correct, the congregation are deeply engaged in these. The tendency of the preacher is to understand and master. They usually move quickly beyond reaction and response to find the 'meaning'. But to move too quickly to a carefully constructed meaning runs the danger of leaving the congregation behind.

> . . . laity come to the Bible expecting to be affected by what they encounter there. Such an effect is not simply, or even primarily, cognitive; it tends to be more aesthetic or emotional. Clergy, however, tend to be more interested in identifying and communicating messages in the text that are both relevant to the present congregation and compatible with the original intention of the author. Given this reality, two types of problem may occur: (1) laity who are prone to construing meaning as

---

10 Mark Allen Powell, 2007, *What Do They Hear? Bridging the Gap between Pulpit and Pew*, Nashville: Abingdon, p. 102.

effect may respond to the text in idiosyncratic ways; and (2) clergy who are inclined to equate meaning with message may end up answering questions that no one was asking.[11]

Being open to the text

Being as open to the text as we can be will open us to the living word of God and let it speak. However, it is not easy to be fully open to texts which are familiar to us and about which we might say 'we know what this is about'.

If the preacher is to offer imaginative alternatives and possibilities in the sermon, creating images for new life and fresh hope, then an imaginative engagement with the text seems a good place to start.

The following two exercises are intended to open up this kind of imaginative response.

Exercise 1

Find a copy of a picture, preferably a painting by an artist you are not familiar with. The internet is a good source for this. A painting rather than a photograph works best because it is clearer that a painting is an imaginative and interpretative work by an artist. (There is an analogy here with the interpretative and imaginative work of an author or editor of a Scripture text.)

The aim is to approach the 'text' (in this case a painting) with openness and imagination.

Look at the picture.
What do you see?
What is your response?
Why do you respond in this way?
What questions would you like to ask the artist?
How might this relate to your response to a Scripture text?

Exercise 2

Choose a passage of Scripture. It is helpful to choose one from the readings for an occasion on which you will be preaching.

Read the Scripture passage with the intention of reacting to it and being open.

---

11 Powell, *What Do They Hear?*, p. 105.

Be attentive to the action of God, and to the unfolding interactions between God and God's people that are the underlying energy in a biblical text.

1. Read the text aloud

   Do this in one or two translations. This will have the effect of returning the text to the medium for which it was first prepared, and in which it was first encountered, whether as a hymn sung in worship, a story recounted to a community, or a letter read out to a waiting congregation. The written form is secondary, the oral form is primary.

2. Try out different voices in the readings

   What difference does it make to the hearing if the voice is earnest? angry? ironic? pleading? compassionate? probing? co-operative? contentious?

   How do these echo the voice that seems to speak from the text?

   > the liberation mood of 'Exodus'
   > the pathos or anger of the prophet
   > the hope of a vision
   > the joy and comfort of God's presence
   > the vulnerability of love
   > the release of mercy and grace

3. Ask the text some 'hard questions'

   - *What catches my eye, my ear, my heart* in the Scripture text especially in light of what is going on in the congregation, the community and culture, in our worship, in me?
   - 'What's *this*?' when you see something curious, perplexing, seemingly irrelevant, utterly mundane, rather off-putting, very unsettling, or even downright sacrilegious.
   - 'That's *crazy*! when it doesn't seem to fit into the bigger biblical picture in which it occurs, when it seems out of sync with what 'everybody knows' about religion!
   - 'Yes, *but . . .*' when what meets the eye makes a certain amount of sense – but on the *other hand*, it surely doesn't seem to be *the whole truth, and nothing but the truth* about what we experience.
   - 'What's *at stake* here?' when the writer, or a character portrayed by the writer, is clearly 'exercised' about what is being said.

What you are doing in all of this is *not* trying to 'master' the text or to 'summarize the truth'. Rather, put yourself in a position to be surprised by the shock of recognition.

The approach described here will cultivate creative theological connections and analogies between the revelatory processes at work in Scripture, culture, congregation, liturgy and preacher.

Try to get out of control instead of figuring out the 'point'!

Once this exercise has been done you will be able to approach commentaries and other resources with the questions you need to ask. They will be an aid to you in the sermon you need to prepare rather than determinative of the content or direction.

Attentive listening

We began this chapter with the claim that preaching is part of a dialogue and the sermon is one voice in an ongoing faithful conversation. An important part of this is attentive listening. The preacher will be attentive and aware of what is going on in the local community and the wider world and will bring this to the sermon preparation. But the preacher also needs to be able to hear the response that people make to the sermon itself and discover how it has contributed to the development of individuals and the congregation. The sermon once delivered has a life in the hearing and understanding of those who have been present at its preaching.

Alongside this it is important to encourage members of the congregation themselves to be attentive and expectant listeners, both to the word of God in Scripture, and to the way that word is broken open in preaching.

If we take seriously the view that the preacher mediates a saving encounter between the believer and the living God, the uncritical response 'nice sermon, vicar' (and its lay equivalent) will not do. We do not preach to elicit feelings of niceness, we preach to allow God's word to be heard as we grow as disciples of Jesus.

In order to help a congregation break the mould of simple consumer response – 'I like this, I don't like that' – and to take responsibility for their own response, the preacher should engender a set of questions that members of the congregation become used to asking of themselves: What did I hear? How did I hear it? What has it left me with? What shall I do?

This can be formalized in a sermon response form and an example of this is given at the end of this chapter. This can also be addressed through questions for home or house groups or through a sermon reflection group drawn together by the preacher. A sermon that is preached but not reflected upon either by the preacher or by the congregation is a sermon that is incomplete. A sermon that is preached without attention to the life of the

Sermon Response Form

Thank you for volunteering to record the response to this sermon.
The preacher will prepare the sermon with care but, as with any sermon, it is what people hear and take away from it that matters and indeed what preaching is all about. Different people will hear the same sermon in different ways and it is helpful for the preacher to understand what *you* have heard in the sermon and what has made an impact.

Name of Preacher ....

Church ....

Date ....

Type of Service...

Reading(s) for the day..

Please fill in this form soon after the service in which the sermon was preached.

What was the message of the sermon? In what ways was this 'good news'?

What thoughts has the sermon left you with?

What might you do as a result of hearing this sermon?

How did the sermon relate to the Scripture reading(s)?

How did the preacher put this message across? How effective was this for you?

How did the sermon begin and end? How effective was this for you?

How might this sermon develop if it was preached again?

In what ways do you think this sermon was suitable for this congregation on this occasion?

community is merely a monologue. A congregation that is not prepared to listen with attentiveness and expectancy is in danger of demanding entertainment instead of the word of God. Preaching and its work in growing the preacher and congregation in discipleship is a shared calling and one that provides opportunity for the Holy Spirit to live in our common life.

Suggested further reading

Walter Brueggemann, 1997, *Cadences of Home: Preaching among Exiles*, Louisville: Westminster John Knox.

D. Day, J. Astley and L. Francis, 2005, *A Reader on Preaching*, Aldershot: Ashgate.

David Day, 2004, *A Preaching Workbook*, London: SPCK.

Susan Durber, 2007, *Preaching Like a Woman*, London: SPCK.

Richard Eslinger, 1995, *Narrative Imagination: Preaching the Worlds that Shape Us*, Minneapolis: Fortress.

Thomas G. Long, 2005, *The Witness of Preaching*, 2nd edn, Louisville: Westminster John Knox.

David Schlafer and Thomas Sedgwick, 2007, *Preaching What We Practice: Proclamation and Moral Discernment*, Harrisburg, PA: Morehouse.

Thomas Troeger, 1990, *Imagining a Sermon*, Nashville: Abingdon.

John W. Wright, 2007, *Telling God's Story, Narrative Preaching for Christian Formation*, Downers Grove, IL: IVP Academic.

10

Money

JOHN PRESTON

Money creates all kinds of preconceptions . . . In embarking on this chapter, the reader might hope to find

- practical advice on how to sustain the income necessary for a parish's mission and ministry
- theological equipping for the priest to grapple with the 'eye of the needle' and to avoid the 'love of money'
- pastoral guidance on working with those in debt
- pointers to resources on financial management for churches
- guidance on preaching about money, giving and generosity.

It will be somewhat easier to disappoint such a wide range of possible expectations than to satisfy them! Although this chapter may prove useful in helping the reader generate the income necessary to sustain and grow a parish's mission and ministry, the principal aim of this chapter is to provide a more holistic overview to the issue of money. For money touches many parts of ministry, and clergy encounter it in a number of different roles.

For some clergy, however, there is little desire to tackle the issue of money. Loren Mead writes:

> Some pastors make a virtue of being 'above' all that concern for filthy lucre . . . Under the rubric that money is 'secular' and that the pastor's work has to do with the 'sacred,' clergy have written a brief that permits them to avoid leadership in the financial management and leadership of the congregation . . . This means that clergy not only give little leadership to the financial life of a congregation, but also set up a climate that sets little value on the functions of financial management carried out by others . . . It means pastoral abdication of one of the most troubling dimensions of living in our society.[1]

---

1 Loren B. Mead, 1998, *Financial Meltdown in the Mainline?*, Hearndon: Alban Institute.

It is the author's observation that the American church culture is more willing to talk about money issues than in the UK, and that Loren Mead's observations do also relate to a number of UK clergy.

Clergy and money

Whether at the beginning of a stipendiary or non-stipendiary ministry, money will play a different role in the life of the priest. Many will need to take time to adjust to new levels of income and different patterns of expenditure.

For the stipendiary, the same 'stipend' is paid to all. While this is supposed to be the amount of money necessary to avoid the priest being distracted from his or her ministry, the reality is probably closer to a salary package as the same amount is paid whether or not the priest has a working partner, and whether or not there are dependants to be cared for. There is no performance pay, and at times it may seem unfair that diligence in pursuit of mission and ministry is rewarded the same in financial terms as colleagues who may appear to be working fewer hours or having less impact in their ministry. In some parishes this will be a relatively small wage in comparison with professional people on large incomes; in others the stipend can feel almost embarrassingly high. Unless the priest is able to come to terms with these inequalities, either of them has the potential to cripple the priest's confidence in working with, and preaching about, money.

Since clergy enter ministry from many different walks of life, there will be a variable degree of adjustment required. Some stipendiary priests will need to adjust to a significantly lower wage than previously received; for others, household income may rise. On a practical point, tax affairs will become significantly more complex, and most new clergy will require tax advice. Another practical point relates to expenses, which will be approved and refunded by the PCC. This will give a level of scrutiny which may at times seem unfair. It is wise to agree policy and practices ahead of issues relating to individual expenses, and suggested models are widely available.

Both stipendiary and non-stipendiary priests may note a difference in how their spending is perceived. The choice of car, the holiday destination, or even choice of supermarket can cause comments in the parish that would not have arisen previously. While spending decisions should not be dictated by others, there is nevertheless a greater visibility, which strengthens the need for accountability for personal stewardship in spending.

It is important to come to be comfortable with money; which is, of course, a different thing from having enough money to live comfortably!

Ideally some quality in-depth thinking will have taken place prior to ordination for those who become stipendiary priests. This needs to embrace
the changes that may need to be made in lifestyle, in spending habits, in
the amount of security that money might offer, and so on.

If you haven't yet become comfortable with money, you might spend
some time discussing this in a supervisory context, or work through the
books by Preston or by Tondeur and Pierce in the Further Reading section
at the end of this chapter.

Reflections:
Simon has come to ministry in his forties after a successful career in
retailing. 'I knew what the score would be, but adjusting to having a
lower income than my wife has taken me some time. Perhaps it's a man
thing, but the passing of the main responsibility for paying the bills really took me by surprise.'

Jenny is a non-stipendiary priest, who continues in secular employment. 'As an NSM, I hadn't thought that anything would change with
regard to money, but I feel it matters more what I choose to do with
my money now I'm a priest.'

Steven has teenage children. 'Sometimes it really hurts that I've given
up the opportunity of earning more, and I feel that I'm depriving my
children of the things that, ideally, I'd like to give them. The sacrifice
isn't always where I expected to be required to make it.'

Many people find it difficult to manage their money, and it is not surprising that a number of clergy struggle with money, and as a result end up
with debts that seem to mount up quickly. Whenever this is the case, it's
vital to take action sooner rather than later. The first step is to ensure
careful budgeting – monitoring what comes in and goes out. If this doesn't
make a sufficient improvement, then professional advice should be sought.
This is available free – the Consumer Credit Counselling service offers free
advice to those in debt. They can be found at www.cccs.co.uk, and there
are some very useful tools available on their website. As clergy are engaged
in public ministry it is important that their money is managed reasonably
well, yet they must retain personal choice in financial matters.

Preachers and money

'It feels like I'm singing for my supper!' is one reason why some clergy find
it uncomfortable to preach about money. Yet the giving of money to the

church is not the main reason why money should be talked about from the pulpit.

How we handle our money, wealth and possessions is primarily a discipleship issue. Rowan Williams once said:

> What we do with our money proclaims who we think we are – whether we know it or not, whether we like it or not. All our actions in some degree reveal us; why should our economic life be different? Why should this too not be an area in which we help to shape our eternal destiny, a matter of sin or holiness?[2]

Put another way, one of the most telling insights into our personal values and priorities is the way we spend our money. What we choose to prioritize, the balance we strike between the different demands on our cash, reveals with a stark clarity what we hold to be most important.

And so, the main aim of the preacher is to equip listeners to be holistically generous – as, for example, was the Good Samaritan in the parable quoted by Luke. In that story, help for neighbour is given through time, personal risk, discomfort in walking alongside the donkey carrying the injured traveller, and finally in money, as the Samaritan pays a local innkeeper for food and lodgings for the injured traveller. Yet most retellings of such stories seem to gloss over the money element. It is as though it was never there. In some way we seem to have stripped money from the Bible – yet a survey shows over 2,000 verses on money, wealth and possessions – many times more than relate to prayer or to faith.

While topics such as consumerism, levels of pension saving or life insurance, personal debt, or other financial issues may seldom be the focus of sermons, these are decisions that church members are having to take regularly. As disciples, our faith should inform the choices we make in our lives, and teaching and preaching need to gently establish sound Christian principles so that church members can become comfortable in applying faith to such topics.

The concept of stewardship is vital to preaching and biblical teaching about money. While it sometimes appears that the church has hijacked the word to relate to giving to the church, stewardship is our response to caring for that which God has entrusted to us – time, skills, money and even God's mission to the world. Good preaching on issues of money and stewardship helps people tackle the issues encountered in daily living.

---

2 Talk given by Archbishop Rowan Williams (then Bishop of Monmouth) to the Stewardship Network.

Some preachers only reluctantly accept the need to talk about money, retaining the mindset of financial need. This gives an inadequate foundation for enabling church members to embrace the stewardship and discipleship aspects.

Preaching about money should not be limited to an annual 'giving sermon'. The lectionary is crowded with passages that relate to money, to God's generous provision, to lifestyle choices that disciples need to make. Routine preaching on these issues as they arise is more helpful than the occasional 'special' sermon, as in itself it demonstrates that teaching on money is integral to other discipleship issues.

Parishes and money

As we shall see in David Parrott's chapter, the PCC is a charity, and its members are trustees, and many priests will find themselves chairing PCCs as a part of their ministry. While the priest as *preacher* is not primarily concerned with meeting the parish's specific needs for mission, the priest as *chair of trustees* of a small to medium sized local charity will lead the PCC in financing its mission and ministry.

Stewardship is often seen as an individual responsibility. But the corporate actions of the church at all levels should also demonstrate the response to the love of a generous God who entrusts us with responsibility for money, for mission and for ministry. Yet often, it seems that a group of individuals who have understood God's provision and their stewardship of it adopt a very different persona when together on the Church Council! This section seeks to consider what it means to be good corporate stewards, and to look at the role of the incumbent as chair of the PCC.

It is important to get the right balance concerning money. We need to be right before God, and right in meeting the proper expectations of our society (2 Cor. 8.16–24). There should be good controls, careful stewardship, and good budgeting, yet without a dominating penny-pinching mentality that belies the abundance of God's provision.[3] Ultimately, the mission and ministry of the church will be enriched or constrained by the generosity of the congregation, and regular teaching and development of generosity are vital, not so much to pay the bills as to widen the expressions of mission and ministry in which the church is able to engage.

A three-year view of money is good practice. Within the current year, it is important to have the monitoring systems and controls in place to

---

3 Walter Brueggemann, 1999, 'The liturgy of abundance, the myth of scarcity', *Christian Century*, 24–31 March.

ensure the church is spending what it expects to spend, and that the implications of unplanned spending (or income!) are worked through. The size of the parish will influence the level of management and control required. What is necessary in a large, complex parish turning over hundreds of thousands of pounds is more than is needed in a small rural parish; but even the smallest church must have basic controls, such as having two people counting the collection or signing cheques.

In the autumn, it is good to develop a budget for the following year. This enables the church to decide in advance what it holds to be important and where it will choose to allocate its expected funds. This will also help the essential work of communication of financial needs and the vision for ministry that the money will underpin. As part of this process, it is also helpful to think a year further ahead (although this will necessarily be a less detailed plan) to plan for major areas of expenditure, or expected changes in income. As part of their stewardship, PCCs also need to work out a reserves policy, whether they are blessed with large financial reserves or none.

The PCC also needs to give proper account of its spending decisions – of how it has used the funds that have been provided to it. The Treasurer will make a report at the APCM, although this will often be a detailed financial report, and perhaps not particularly engaging. Alongside this it is recommended that the PCC link giving with the charitable outcomes that have flowed from the giving. The wider charitable sector has become very good at helping donors envisage the benefit that their giving will lead to – that a goat might be provided for a family in a developing country, or that a child can be sponsored for a month to receive education and food, or that an orphanage can be funded for a week and so on. All too often the church has simply spoken about costs, rather than helping people to see the activities, and particularly the impact on people's lives, that flow from this.

There are many possible mission and ministry outcomes that a church might describe:

- shaping emerging spiritual values through primary school assemblies
- enabling people visiting the churchyard to find space and inner peace
- time invested ministering to grieving families
- people coming to a living faith through enquirer and evangelism courses
- enabling children and young people to feel valued and to grow spiritually through dedicated activities.

And so on. What would your list look like?

There may be a reluctance to 'blow our own trumpet', but if we can set this appropriately within a stewardship context, it is good accountability to explain how the money that has been donated to the church has been used to achieve charitable impact. It also equips church members with the insight to help divide their giving between their local church and the other causes and charities that build God's kingdom.

This linking of giving with the mission and ministry outcomes that flow from it, is one of four key tasks outlined in the General Synod report *Giving for Life*.[4] The others are:

- Preach and teach holistically about money, and to do so in the context of discipleship.
- To send a thank you letter to donors once a year, which also offers an opportunity to reiterate the outcomes that we have considered above. It is wise to resist the temptation to add a 'P. S.' – that inflation has been at work, and we now need increased levels of giving to maintain the church's work – as this devalues the thank you.
- To conduct some form of annual review that will provide church members with the opportunity to review their giving. This will undoubtedly need to take a different form each year, to avoid staleness. One year might focus on a personal reflection, and lead to pledges for individuals giving to the church; another year might have a teaching or home group programme on a more holistic view of money or giving. Year 3 might revert to a pledge-based programme, and Year 4 might have a discipleship or a thanksgiving and worship focus.

The Stewardship Year	
January	As the church starts its new financial year, it is a good time to thank regular givers for their giving, and to remind them what their giving achieves.
March/April	The Annual Parochial Church Meeting is an important time to communicate how the church has used the money given to it.
May/June	A good time for an annual giving review. This could also be in the autumn, linked to the church's budget.
September/ Harvest	Thanksgiving is a natural time to focus on God's generosity to us.
September to November	Developing and agreeing a budget for the forthcoming year.

4 *Giving for Life* (GS 1723). London: Church of England General Synod, 2009.

Many parishes have found it helpful to appoint someone who can lead this work. This person, together with those who preach and teach, can play a significant role in resourcing the parish's mission and ministry. Many dioceses support such a network, albeit with varying titles, and there are a range of resources to support this on the Parish Resources website.[5]

Before concluding this section on the parish and money, it is worth pausing to reflect on the power that money creates, and the potential to abuse that power. While the majority of parish treasurers serve as wise stewards, some parishes have been constrained in their ministry by treasurers or others whose fear of scarcity or personal agendas have dominated money discussions, seeking to persuade the PCC that certain things cannot be afforded, while funding can be found for others. One of the advantages of budgeting is that this encourages wider PCC ownership of decisions around priorities, and to some degree neutralizes the potential for the abuse of power by any one individual.

Pastors and money

The attentive priest will also find money appearing as part of pastoral encounters, often behind the presenting problem. It is vital that clergy are comfortable with money talk and their own situation, if they are to be open to others. Some clergy are provided with a hardship fund by their parish, and prayer-informed wisdom is needed to allocate this wisely. Such a fund can be important as there are few sources of funds that can be applied quickly and discreetly. It is important that gifts out of such a fund do make a difference, even if that difference is short term, yet the extent of the gift should not be such that undue favour has been seen to be applied.

In 2009, the Church of England launched a 'Matter of Life and Debt' campaign to raise awareness of the issue of debt. Support for the campaign in the national media was far greater than expected, and it attracted widespread comment. The response from the financial sector was uncertain though there was a broad welcome for the Church's involvement. In essence, the message was 'we're able to help with sorting out the financial issues, but alongside these we often find issues that you in the church call "pastoral", and we're not really qualified to help with those'. Very often it is some unanticipated change in personal circumstances, such as illness, redundancy or bereavement, that can change an individual's ability to manage levels of debt; taking them from just about coping into a situation where the debt is spiralling out of control.

5 www.parishresources.org.uk.

Another aspect of the pastor's encounter with money will relate to encounters with those struggling with debt. There may be a perception that the Church is not interested in helping people who have money problems, and a side benefit of preaching and teaching on a wide range of money topics is that it gives permission to people to raise these issues. It is a good idea to display a small card or poster on the church notice board advertising free debt counselling from the Consumer Credit Counselling Service (CCCS) or local Citizens Advice Bureau, Christians Against Poverty or some other good local advice centre. As well as providing a pointer to those in need of the service, this also indicates that this is a subject with which the Church is willing to engage.

There is plenty of professional, skilled help available without charge (e.g. http://www.cccs.co.uk/) and clergy are encouraged to acquaint themselves with where such help can be found before it is needed. The help that the pastor can give is likely to be found in two areas. First, encouraging those with serious debts to engage with the issue, and second, if necessary, providing pastoral support while debt counselling is undertaken, or the outcomes of it worked through.

The plate and money

The final encounter with money considered here is that of the role of money in worship. In most Anglican churches there is a strange custom that half way through the service, under cover of a hymn, two (or more) sidespeople will pass around a bag or plate to receive donations. This can take the newcomer by surprise – so this is what 'offertory hymn' means, and a quick lunge into the pocket can produce a coin or two. Surprisingly the newcomer notes a number of people, who are surely regulars, ignoring the bag completely, unaware that they may be giving by regular standing order. Is this strange custom only for newcomers?!

Given the added challenge of getting a gift-aid declaration on this kind of giving, this is clearly not a good fundraising technique. So something else is going on.

It seems that we have in many places lost the connection between the offering of our money, and our remembering of Christ's sacrificial offering in the Eucharist. That the money and the bread and wine are brought up together is no coincidence, no attempt to reduce the number of interruptions to the service. Since money represents us in a way that nothing else can, it is the offering of money that is the closest proxy we can have to offering ourselves. As the service moves from the liturgy of the word into the liturgy of sacrament, the offering of ourselves is represented by the gift of money, as we then remember the offering of Christ as we receive the bread and wine.

At this point in our worship, this 'sacrament' of giving has very little to do with the financial needs of the church. It is not primarily a response to an appeal for funds, or to the need to finance programmes and ministries, but rather that as we give, we are caught up in a response to God's grace. We give because we have a need to give, in response and in thanks for all that God has given to us. It matters little that the nature of our response is inevitably inadequate – this is so whether we give a pound, a tithe or a double tithe. What is important is that our hearts are sincere, and that our offering is precisely that, an offering which reflects and represents what God has given to us.

There is more than a semantic difference between 'receiving an offering' and 'taking a collection', and it is good to sometimes vary the practice that a parish church adopts; perhaps receiving the offering in silence one week, or introducing it occasionally to remind people of its purpose and role in worship. It is also important to include in this offering the gifts of those that have given directly through bank accounts.

Summary

In and of itself, money is neither good nor bad! The love of money is described as 'a root of all kinds of evil' (1 Tim. 6.10) but the stewardship opportunity that comes with it is a positive opportunity to live out our faith. Money is a complex issue, and needs time and reflection allocated to it to ensure that the deeply personal issues that may exist are faced, and that it is understood as a spiritual subject that touches many aspects of ministry, personal lifestyles, church administration, and the resourcing of mission as well as the offering of ourselves in worship.

Suggested further reading

Stuart Murray, 2002, *Beyond Tithing*, Carlisle: Paternoster Press.
Martyn Percy, 2006, *Clergy: The Origin of Species*, London: Continuum.
Parish Resources website: www.parishresources.org.uk.
John Preston, 2007, *The Money Revolution*, Carlisle: Authentic Media.
Peter Selby, 2009, *Grace and Mortgage*, London: Darton, Longman and Todd.
Keith Tondeur and Steve Pierce, 2010, *Your Money and Your Life*, revised edn, London: SPCK.

11

Law

DAVID PARROTT

Why does a church need law?

For many people this is the starting point when considering how law works and its impact on ministry. Without some understanding of why we have law it is hard to move into understanding what else a minister needs to know. I shall answer the question by giving two reasons and two myths.

The first reason the Church needs law is that every organization of any sort throughout history has had to develop rules for itself. The reason for this is that relationship requires regulation if it is to be healthy. Put the other way around, all laws basically regulate relationships. Let me give some examples.

Family law governs the relationship between family members in good times and in bad. Civil law governs the relationships we have with our neighbours and those we interact with day by day. Contract law governs the relationship between two parties who agree a lawful transaction. Criminal law governs the actions of those who step outside the bounds of what society says is appropriate behaviour towards others and their property. It follows that church law governs the relationships of members of the Church to one another and to those outside the Church.

The second reason that the Church has laws is found in the Bible. The Old Testament is full of law. From the time of creation (You shall not eat from the tree of life), through the laws given to the people of Israel (the ten commandments and all the laws regulating society) the covenant relationship between God and his people has always been regulated by law. Matthew 5.17 reports Jesus saying 'Do not think that I have come to abolish the law . . .', but we would say that his interpretation of the law is less 'legalistic' and is more concerned with general rules and intention ('you have heard that it was said . . . but I say to you . . .', verses 21–48). Within Paul's epistles we see a great concern with law and order; the picture that we see in the epistles and elsewhere in the New Testament is of a church that is becoming structured and ordered. Historically, the Church has always had laws which regulate its life and relationships, and the Church of England is no different.

Yet, despite the above two reasons, the Church has always had those who object to laws. Hence I want to explore the two most common myths. My response to both myths is: have you not read your Bible?

The first myth is this: we have the Holy Spirit; his guidance is enough. My response to this is: didn't they try this in Corinth and elsewhere? Yet Paul needed swiftly to set some guidelines and boundaries. To put it simply, when Paul explores the relationship between the flesh and the Spirit he concludes that we will not know perfection until we are in heaven. So for the time being we need some laws to live by.

The second great myth is expressed like this: isn't love enough? If we are truly a people of love we will not need law. But as Paul reminds us in Romans, love needs a context. Love is the fulfilling of the law, he says (Rom. 13.10), not the disposal of it. It simply is not good enough to use these two myths to seek to avoid the need for church law. Rather we need to understand where our own church law comes from, and to know its purpose and practice, so that we can be part of the loving spiritual order which the Church should have.

How does the Church get different types of law?

In the Church of England, law can be made in several ways. The most significant laws are passed by General Synod in the form of measures. These are sometimes called primary legislation. A measure is sent by Synod to Parliament for scrutiny and then receives the royal assent. Measures have the same effect and authority as Acts of Parliament. Measures can apply to anyone affected by their particular subject matter, whether they are members of the church or not. Other forms of legislation include canons, schemes, orders and other instruments, which generally have the same force as parliamentary Statutory Instruments. The doctrinal and liturgical documents also have the effect of being church laws and the Thirty-Nine Articles, Book of Common Prayer and *Common Worship* services contain rules and directions (often called rubrics) which must be followed.

There is another body of rules which hold a different status from these primary laws. These are sometimes known as quasi-legislation. This category includes regulations, codes of practice, circulars and guidelines issued either by the central church or by diocesan authorities. These do not have the same authority as measures and canons but it is generally assumed that most of this legislation would be enforceable and, therefore, should be obeyed. All of this church law sits within the historic common law of the Church of England known as the *jus commune*. This consists of the laws and customs of the Church pre-dating the specific canon law and ecclesiastical law of the modern church.[1]

What is the purpose of church law?

Is there a common purpose for church law? In the study of any academic subject it is usual that there will be those who analyse what is going on under the surface and come up with a theory about it. This is also true of church law. Historically there have been two theoretical approaches to understanding the purpose of church law. These have sometimes been called the facility theory and the order theory. In the facility theory the understanding is that the purpose of law is to empower and enable the Church to fulfil its calling. Law is there to facilitate the Church's mission. A recent example of Church of England law which would fit this theory is the Dioceses, Pastoral and Mission Measure 2007, which seeks to enable new mission initiatives so that the structures of the church are mission-oriented.

The second theory is called the order theory. Here the suggestion is that the purpose of church law is to ensure order in the Church. The law creates institutions, offices and boundaries in order that its mission may be properly fulfilled. Again there is an obvious modern example of this in Church of England law. The Clergy Discipline Measure 2003 sets out what is acceptable and unacceptable behaviour for the Church's authorized ministers.

Academics love to study their subject and conclude that it is one thing or another. It is clear that the law in the Church of England seeks to span both these theories, but together they seem to give a good working model to help us understand the purpose of church law.

Who enforces law?

The first and most important answer to this question is you! To some extent, by virtue of being an authorized minister of the Church, you are now a church lawyer. You will be required to know, understand and put into practice church law. But there are also others who have more specific responsibilities.

---

1 See David Parrott, 2011, *Your Church and the Law*, Norwich: Canterbury Press, chapter 2.

First there is the chancellor. He or she is the judge of the bishop's diocesan court and makes decisions on a range of matters. Most people come across the chancellor when they need to seek permission to do repairs or make changes to the church building. The chancellor is the person whose permission facilitates that part of our work (hence the name faculty). Next there is an officer called the registrar. This person acts as the bishop's legal advisor and as administrator of the chancellor's court. The bishop is often called on to make legal decisions. A range of church law states that in cases of doubt or dispute the bishop will make the final decision, so he too enforces the law on many occasions. Finally there is the archdeacon. He or she will often be the first port of call when a difficult legal question arises.

Why do I need to know about the law?

One of the leading Roman Catholic canonists, James A. Coriden, writes, 'Canon law shapes and guides the life of the church in many ways. For those who care about the church, it is important to understand its rules.'[2] This statement, it seems to me, sums up the answer to the question of why we need laws: because we love the Church. If we are to be people who know the boundaries of what is right and wrong, what is good and bad, what is appropriate and inappropriate, then we need some laws which set this out.

You have been asked to explore ways in which the church can be more child friendly. You decide with the small planning group that if you moved three pews from the north aisle of the church you would be able to create a children's corner, which could be carpeted and have soft toys available. Is there any problem?

Clergy sometimes say to me: 'I am more interested in mission than in structures and law.' My response is always the same: 'You are part of a law-based church. You agreed to that, both at your ordination and at the time of each appointment. If you are serious about mission, why would you want to waste your time repeating anything other than mission?' I know so many clergy and PCCs who plan some parish project or another, only to discover that they have to start again when they find the legal boundaries prevent them from doing what they had planned. If they had taken the trouble to know a little church law to start with, they would not have wasted their valuable mission time by having to do the administrative and legal work twice. The same is true of anyone with responsibility

2 James A. Coriden, 2011, *An Introduction to Canon Law*, London: Continuum, p. 6.

in the Church. If we are serious about mission in the Church of England, we need to know the rules of the organization we swore to uphold, so that we can work within their boundaries as easily as possible and not waste our time making mistakes which could have been avoided.

What do I need to know?

It seems to me that there are two basic principles that will stand you in good stead when it comes to dealing with church law. The first I call the 'alarm bell principle'. That is to say, you need to know when there is a question to ask. You will not be able to learn all that there is to know about church law. But you need to know enough so that your alarm bells ring at the right moment and you can look up the information and get the answer. Your task is to know when to ask the right question.

> The vicar decides that he will change the services used on different Sundays of each month. He tells you that it is his right to decide. Is he correct?

The second principle is what I call the 'white charger principle'. Clergy often think that they know what is the right thing for their church and their congregation. They then seek to move forward into that future, not having asked the right questions. When they are challenged, their first reaction is to get on their white charger and defend their position. My advice is this: don't waste your time defending the indefensible. If you know just enough about church law, and discover that you are wrong, back down and look for a new way forward. Many clergy have wasted long hours on their white charger, defending what is in fact wrong in law, and that is a simple waste of time and energy.

Having said you will not be able to learn all that there is to know about church law, let me give three short examples of areas of church law where you will need some knowledge. You will find more details on these and other subjects in the resources at the end of this chapter.

Worship[3]

In this area I would suggest that there are three things you most need to know. Who decides what services are to be used in a church? What

---

3   For further detail see Parrott, *Your Church and the Law*, chapter 15.

are authorized and commended services? How do I deal with copyright law?

Who decides on the form of service?

Decisions as to which of the authorized forms of service (including the Book of Common Prayer) are to be used in any church in a parish (other than the services for occasional offices) must be taken jointly by the minister and the PCC. Note that this is simple and absolute. Many clergy believe that they can decide, but that is not the case.

The answer is slightly different for occasional offices (other than confirmation, where the bishop decides). The decision as to which form of service is to be used is made by the minister who is to conduct the service, but if the people concerned object beforehand to the use of the service selected by the minister and they cannot agree, the matter must be referred to the bishop for his decision.

What services may be used?

The General Synod of the Church of England is permitted to authorize services in addition to the Book of Common Prayer, which remains the norm for all services if authorized alternatives are not used. Ministers must use only the forms of service authorized by canon, although they have limited discretion to make minor changes within authorized services. It is the minister's responsibility to have a good understanding of the forms of service used and to ensure that the worship offered glorifies God and enlightens the people.

In today's church there is a wide range of liturgical material available, and this falls into two categories: authorized services and commended services. Authorized services have been approved by General Synod. Commended services are resources which the House of Bishops has indicated they would deem to fit within the authorized patterns of worship (especially that called the Service of the Word in *Common Worship*). Full lists of these services are available among the resources at the end of the chapter.

Copyright

It is often the case, especially since the introduction of *Common Worship*, that a parish will wish to prepare service booklets or leaflets for general use or for a specific occasion. There is a very useful leaflet setting out all the requirements for such materials called *A Brief Guide to Liturgical*

Copyright. Liturgical Texts for Local Use: Copyright Information. This is
available from the Church of England website. Copyright permission over
music can be obtained via Christian Copyright Licensing (Europe) Ltd.

PCC[4]

All clergy, no matter how new to the
role, need to know something about
the PCC. You will be a member,
whether you like it or not, so it's best
to learn something about it. I think
that there are three things you most
need to know. What are the functions of the PCC? Who is a member
of the PCC? What happens at PCC
meetings? The rules and regulations
regarding PCCs are set out in the
Church Representation Rules.

> The Vicar wants to stand
> aside from the chairmanship
> of a particular PCC meeting
> so that she can work to get
> her motion passed, against
> some opposition. She asks
> you to chair the meeting, as
> the Vice Chairman is one of
> the people who objects to
> her proposal. Can you?

Annual Meetings (APCM) are usually the responsibility of the incumbent, so we shall not cover that subject here, though on both subjects there
are plenty of more detailed resources available for your assistance.

Functions and purpose of the PCC

It is the duty of the minister and the PCC to consult together on matters
of general concern and importance to the parish. The PCC is a body corporate in its own right; in other words it has a legal status to which attach
certain rights and duties.

The functions of a PCC include:

* co-operation with the minister in promoting in the parish the whole
  mission of the church, pastoral, evangelistic, social and ecumenical;
* the consideration and discussions of any matters concerning the
  Church of England or of religious or public interest;
* making known and putting into effect any provision made by the
  diocesan synod or the deanery synod;
* giving advice to the diocesan synod and the deanery synod on any
  matter referred to the council;

---

4 For further detail see Parrott, *Your Church and the Law*, ch. 5.

- raising such matters as the council consider appropriate with the diocesan synod or deanery synod.

A senior Law Lord recently commented:

The key to the role of the PCC lies in the first of its general functions: co-operation with the minister in promoting in the parish the whole mission of the church. Its other more particular functions are to be seen as ways of carrying out this general function.[5]

The functions of the PCC are set out in more detail elsewhere, but briefly other powers, rights and responsibilities of the PCC include:

- responsibility for the financial affairs of the church;
- responsibility for the care, maintenance, preservation and insurance of the fabric of the church and its goods and ornaments;
- responsibility for the care and maintenance of any churchyard;
- power to make representations to the bishop on any matter affecting the welfare of the church in the parish;
- the right to decide, jointly with the incumbent, on the form of service to be used.

Membership of the PCC

The PCC consists of:

- all clerks in Holy Orders beneficed in or licensed to the parish;
- any deaconess or lay worker licensed to the parish;
- in the case of a team ministry, all the members of the team;
- the churchwardens;
- such Readers of the parish as the APCM may determine;
- anyone whose names are on the roll of the parish and who are lay members of any deanery synod, diocesan synod or the General Synod;
- elected lay representatives;
- co-opted members, if the PCC so decides, not exceeding in number one-fifth of the representatives of the elected laity or two persons, whichever is the greater.

---

5 *Lord Rodger of Earlsferry, Aston Cantlow and Wilmcote with Billesley PCC v Wallbank* [2004] 1 AC 546, [2003] 3 All ER 1213, HL, at para. 156.

The rules set out the number of elected members to be on a PCC, as follows:

Number on electoral roll	Number of representatives
0–49	6
50–99	9
100–199	12
200 or more	15

These figures represent the number of elected representatives, not the total size of the PCC, which may be significantly higher. There is provision for the number of elected members to be changed from those in this table. The number of elected representatives may be changed by a resolution passed at any APCM, which will take effect at the next APCM. In order to work with a body whose size is appropriate to the local setting and representative of the parish it may well be appropriate for either the PCC or the standing committee to propose alternative figures to the APCM for it to consider. Unless such a resolution is passed the figures in the table apply.

PCC meetings

The Church Representation Rules set out general provisions relating to PCC meetings. These include provisions regarding the officers of the council, the frequency of meetings, the power to call meetings, notice required for a meeting, chairman of the meetings, quorum, agenda and order of business, place of meetings, voting at meetings, minutes, committees of the PCC and the validity of proceedings.

Common Tenure[6]

From early 2011 all clergy who are appointed to a new post are subject to the terms of service known as Common Tenure. However, not everyone will move into this new process at the same time. For a while the Church of England will have (so to speak) a mixed economy of terms of service. Some post-holders transferred onto Common Tenure automatically. This will include assistant curates, priests-in-charge, team vicars, and residentiary canons on fixed-term appointments, whether in receipt of stipend or not. All other clergy with the freehold (including incumbents, team rectors, deans, archdeacons, and residentiary canons not on fixed-term

---

6 For further detail see Parrott, *Your Church and the Law*, chapter 10.

appointments) were invited around that date to transfer onto common tenure. Some will have done so and others will not. These clergy remain on their existing terms, unless and until they agree to move onto common tenure (which they may do at any time) or leave their current post. There are also a very small number of clergy who have been in a single post since before the early 1970s who hold their posts in a different way.

Freehold

Those who held freehold posts (mainly incumbents) and who chose not to move to common tenure in 2011 will retain the same rights as they had up to that date. A comparison of how the terms of service for freehold differ from common tenure is available on the Church of England website, but for the most part the future is in common tenure. This section will focus on the terms of service in common tenure. The point about common tenure is that it brings with it rights and responsibilities. These did not exist with any clarity in the past.

Common tenure – rights

Common tenure will give to post-holders the following rights:

- an entitlement to be provided with a written statement of particulars setting out the terms of their appointment;
- an entitlement to an uninterrupted rest period of not less than 24 hours in any period of seven days;
- an entitlement to 36 days' annual leave;

> Your curacy is not going well. It seems to you that the Rector makes everything you do seem trivial and even wrong, and you feel that you are learning nothing. What are your options?

- an entitlement to maternity, paternity, parental and adoption leave in accordance with directions given by the Archbishops' Council as Central Stipends Authority;
- an entitlement to request time off, or adjustments to the duties of the office, to care for dependants in accordance with directions given by the Archbishops' Council as Central Stipends Authority;
- an entitlement to spend time on certain public duties other than the duties of the office, with the matter being determined by the bishop if there is any dispute;
- access to a grievance procedure;

- a right of appeal to an employment tribunal if removed from office on grounds of capability;
- the right to accommodation 'reasonably suitable for the purpose', if appropriate.

Common tenure – responsibilities of clergy

The other side of the coin is that clergy will also have some responsibilities and obligations under common tenure. These are:

- to participate and co-operate in ministerial development review (MDR);
- to participate in arrangements approved by the diocesan bishop for continuing ministerial education (CME);
- to inform a person nominated by the bishop when unable to perform the duties of office through sickness;
- to undergo a medical examination where the bishop has reasonable grounds for concern about the office-holder's physical or mental health.

Common tenure – the bishop's responsibility

In order that the clergy are able to fulfil the above there are certain duties imposed on the bishop. These include:

- to make and keep under review a MDR scheme containing arrangements for a person nominated by the bishop to conduct a review with each office-holder in the diocese at least once every two years;
- to use reasonable endeavours to ensure that office-holders in the diocese are afforded opportunities to participate in CME that is appropriate for their ministerial development;
- to have regard to the Archbishops' Council's codes of practice concerning the capability and grievance procedures.

The most important changes in the rights and responsibilities relate to MDR and CME. The new culture created by common tenure means that clergy will be expected to take part in both review and development and this can only be a good thing. However, the part which looks most unlike anything which has existed in the past is the new process of a capability procedure and a grievance procedure.

The principal objective of a capability procedure is to help office-holders whose performance falls below an acceptable minimum standard to improve in cases where the problems are not disciplinary in nature. It is expected that most performance-related matters will be identified and addressed informally without engaging this procedure. However, there is a possibility that the office-holder can be removed from his or her current office under the capability procedure.

In addition to the capability procedure there is also a new grievance procedure. Reconciliation should be the desired outcome and mediation is encouraged. The procedure sets out a range of areas in which a clergyperson may wish to raise a grievance such as the terms of service under which they work, or the MDR or CME processes.

What will I need to know about in the future?

In the above section are just three examples of some of the areas of law you will need to know a little about. Remember, you don't need to know it all, just enough to help you to know when a question needs to be looked at more closely. The range of subjects on which you may need this principle to apply is wide. If, for example, you look at the subjects covered in *Your Church and the Law* you will see that it includes:

Churchwardens, APCMs, PCCs, Baptisms, Marriage, Funerals and Churchyards, Clergy, Clergy Appointments and Terms of Service, Clergy Discipline, Reader Ministry, Rural Deans, Faculties, Worship, Parish Finance, Ecumenism, Employing Staff, Working with Volunteers, Safeguarding Children and Adults, Health and Safety and Data Protection.

This list includes what may be called internal law (law which provides mainly for the regulation of internal church matters) and public law (law which applies to everyone in the land and therefore applies to churches).

Where can I get more help?

There are many places and people you can turn to for help when you need it. Mention has already been made of the archdeacon and the diocesan registrar. They will try to help you when they can, but don't be afraid to do a little work yourself first: you are likely to learn more that way. Explore diocesan and national church websites. Get the right books on your shelf so that you can help yourself. And perhaps the most neglected resource: ask your colleagues, especially those who have been in full-time ministry for many years, or your rural dean. They will often carry a vast amount of information which they have learned along the way.

Why does any of this matter?

I firmly believe that church law matters. It brings order and facilitates our mission and evangelism. But whenever I teach church law to clergy I always end in the same way: with a reminder. Following every law of the church to the letter may make you the best friend of your archdeacon, but it will not ultimately be the making or breaking of your ministry. That will be the result of other things including your own discipleship and your own emotional self-awareness. In my time working as a CME officer I came to the conclusion that these were the two most important factors which sustained and enlivened ministry, and conversely it was specifically a lack of these two things which caused ministries to crumble.

A general lack of knowledge of the law may well cause you endless problems, but in most cases it will not wreck your ministry. A lack of discipleship in your own life, and a low sense of emotional awareness, will be significantly more undermining. Work at these two things above all else – but spare a thought for learning about the wonderful subject of church law!

Resource list

Brief Guide to Liturgical Copyright: Liturgical Texts for Local Use: Copyright Information, 2000, 3rd edn, London: Church House Publishing.

James Behrens, 2005, *Practical Church Management*, 2nd edn, Leominster: Gracewing.

Canons of the Church of England, 2000, London: Church House Publishing.

Church Representation Rules, 2011, London: Church House Publishing.

Martin Dudley and Virginia Rounding, 2003, *Churchwardens: A Survival Guide*, London: SPCK.

Guidelines for the Professional Conduct of the Clergy, 2003, London: Church House Publishing.

Kenneth M. Macmorran and Timothy Briden, 2007, *Handbook for Churchwardens and Parochial Church Councillors*, London: Continuum.

David Parrott, 2011, *Your Church and the Law,* 2nd edn, Norwich: Canterbury Press.

John Pitchford, 2008, *ABC for the PCC: A Handbook for Church Council Members*, London: Continuum.

Lindsay Yates and Will Adam, 2007, *Canon Law and the Newly Ordained*, London: Church House Publishing, 2007.

I 2

Chairing Meetings

NEIL EVANS

Introduction

Have you ever been in one of those meetings that brings about the same reaction as hearing a reading of Azgoth poetry (Douglas Adams in *The Hitchhiker's Guide to the Galaxy* says that one listener survived only by gnawing off one of his own legs)? Perhaps if you have been in that sort of a meeting you may have wondered for a moment what, exactly, it was about the occasion that made it so deadly dull/boring/frustrating. Meetings evoke a whole range of emotions among those attending and those asked to attend, and perhaps the emotion we dread from another person more than anything else is that of excitement. Who can possibly admit to enjoying meetings?

Well, I will admit to being a heretic. I actually believe that meetings can be constructive, interesting, entertaining and fruitful occasions. However, I will also say that I have attended very many meeting which were none of these things! Probably the main reason why so many meetings are the latter is quite simple: no one (and particularly not the chair) has asked, what is this meeting *really* for? Not, what's on the agenda? But, what is the fundamental purpose of this meeting?

We tend to think of meetings as a relatively recent construct, and perhaps they are in their present format, but people have met together for a wide variety of purposes for thousands of years. And every time a group of humans meet there are basically two things going on: a task or collection of tasks and the developing of relationships. I share a meal with family or friends to eat food (task) and to share conversation (develop our relationship). There is content and there is process; the accepted reason why we meet (the church meeting) and the dynamics among the group of people meeting. The combination of these two factors provide for a 'Meeting'.

For the purposes of this chapter I am, of course, going to discuss what by convention we talk of as a 'Meeting' (business meetings). In church terms this means Parochial Church Council or equivalent statutory congregational meetings; other meetings include Standing Committee, Finance and Fabric, Mission and Outreach, Social, Pastoral Committee, etc. However, I will be exploring these in the clear context of the fact that every organization and institution has meetings, and also that whenever two or three meet together, they are a 'Meeting'. Basically, then, I would describe a meeting as a group of people meeting together for a purpose (which may or may not be an agreed purpose).

Jesus had meetings

The Bible is littered with meetings. Jesus had meetings with all sorts of people, from Pharisees to publicans, from his disciples to crowds of 5,000. Sometimes the purpose of the meeting was very clear, with a clearly expressed agenda – take the proclaiming of his vision in the synagogue (Luke 4.16–19), for example – and at other times it was much more obscure, as with the encounter with the Samaritan woman at Jacob's well (John 4.6–30).

The meal Jesus went to with Simon the Pharisee (Luke 7.36–45) is an example of a meeting which went horribly wrong – so far as the 'chair' and agenda setter was concerned! It seems very likely that Simon had a well-formulated agenda for this meeting, but the dynamics of the woman with the ointment and the reaction of Jesus completely hijacked the agenda.

We could draw out any number of other 'meetings' – people meeting together for a purpose – in the Bible, from the meetings of Moses with Pharaoh, of Saul and of David, of Nehemiah and of the prophets, through to Paul's meetings with the various churches recounted in his letters. But perhaps one stands out more than others as being particularly current in its dynamics: the choosing of the first deacons in Acts 6. I invite you to explore and reflect on this passage in the light of this chapter. Note the clarity of agenda, the division and factions, the clear decision-making process and the unexpected outcome. Imagine yourself into what is probably the first recorded council meeting of the Christian Church!

Effective meetings

Being clear about the purpose of a meeting and being real about the interactions of those present are two key elements in leading effective meetings. I propose though that there are four main areas which need major consideration for meetings to be both effective and fruitful. These are purpose, preparation, practicalities and people.

Perhaps the worst meeting I remember attending was run by a church-based community worker when I was vicar in Hackney. He invited several local clergy to a meeting in his office, arriving late himself so we were all waiting outside in the rain. When the meeting did eventually start (all terribly jolly, but no apology), it was clear that he had no real picture of what the purpose of the meeting was; rather he felt he ought to talk to the local clergy, because he was employed by the church. As the meeting progressed in this tiny, untidy room, with one of us perched on a broken chair, we were interrupted on several occasions by his telephone which he answered and then got involved in long conversations. By the end of the meeting, it became apparent that he knew what he wanted to do, having told us in no uncertain terms how important he was and our only use was to do some of his work for him!

If John Cleese had set up such a meeting, it would have seemed too far-fetched. There was no clear purpose; zero preparation had taken place; no consideration had been made for the practical arrangements of the meeting. But probably the worst outcome was, because of the way we clergy had felt treated, he lost significant credibility in our eyes and thereby significantly undermined his own position and possibilities of co-operation.

Although it's easy to set up a meeting badly, it's actually really rather easy to set one up well if a few careful guidelines are followed. Before continuing you might want to consider an outstanding meeting you have attended and a poor one, and to ask what the significant factors at work in both were.

Purpose

Clarity of purpose is far more than just being clear about what's on the agenda – though being clear about what's on the agenda, and ensuring everyone else is clear, is a very good start. Clarity of purpose will include:

- for whose benefit are we meeting?
- what are we hoping to get out of this meeting?
- what is the overall vision for the group we are meeting with?
- how does this meeting fit in with other meetings?

Time spent at the beginning of any meeting clarifying the context can pay great dividends; it will encourage ownership and engagement by those present. Frequently I have attended meetings which promote acquiescence rather than engagement, where people do not feel any ownership of discussion or decisions made.

Statutory meetings: A Church of England Parochial Church Council, for example

Why, then, does the PCC meet? If the only reason is because of a statutory requirement, then everyone's time is being wasted. The meeting will only become real, effective and fruitful where relationships are being developed and where clear tasks are being undertaken; both elements will need constant attention. However, every so often (perhaps once a year after the Annual Meeting) it is worth returning to first principles and reminding everyone why the PCC exists. Three fundamental purposes of the PCC could be expressed as

- vision generation;
- load bearing;
- policy making.

However, far better get the PCC to define it in a way that is appropriate for them. The first meeting of a new PCC would always be for me a fairly quick election of church officers followed by a rather more relaxed and informal review of 'where we are and where are we going'. It's a great opportunity to introduce new members to the work of the PCC while reminding everyone of fundamental principles and purposes. It can be done in a whole variety of ways, by using individuals' stories ('What was the most important thing that happened in the PCC last year?'); by small group discussion (simply, 'What is the PCC for?'); by a hopes and concerns exercise or a 'SWOT' exercise (Strengths/Weaknesses/Opportunities/Threats). The important thing is to tease out of the group why they think they're there and to match that up with an overall vision and reality of what the meeting is for.

Lying behind all deliberations and decisions of the PCC will, therefore, be an overriding purpose. To find ways of expressing this purpose and constantly remind members of 'why we are here' will give a meaningful shape to meetings. It will also be a vital reference point to keep people on track at meetings. Referring back to an agreed statement of purpose is a very useful way of deflecting red herrings and personal hobby-horses.

Discussing and agreeing the fundamental purpose presents an ideal opportunity also to agree (and to challenge) accepted norms of behaviour, values and assumptions. This might include the necessity of actively listening to each other or agreeing that we lay down the 'good old days' and speak rather of today's realities. (Allowing older members a safe place to story-tell can be productive, if it can then be agreed that these stories are laid down.)

I had a discussion with a PCC about the nature of active listening, and undertook a listening exercise with them. It was remarkable to see the penny drop with the majority that they didn't need to put up with one or two people dominating the meeting with boring monologues. This in turn gave permission to the PCC chair to politely shut the bores up as she knew that she had the support of the vast majority. Relationships were developed, the tasks more easily achieved, and, although there was some pain, the meeting became more effective and fruitful.

In discussing purpose it will also be important to have absolute clarity on how this meeting relates to other meetings. So, if there is a Ministry Leadership Team or a regular Staff Meeting everyone needs to know (and agree) how each relates to the other. There are no clear rules for this as each will work differently, but clarity is vital, followed by consistency in the outworking of such relationships. So many disagreements can stem from lack of clarity or inconsistency of approach, with people perceiving that decisions are being made in the wrong place or that they are being inappropriately excluded from decision-making processes.

Similarly there needs to be clarity with sub-groups and subcommittees. How much authority do they have? How does reporting back take place? How is membership decided? At the end of this chapter I give examples of four different types commonly found in churches.

What will also be important is that the structure suits the size and the needs of a particular parish. Clearly a church with a congregation of 30 or 40 will struggle to maintain subcommittees and they will certainly be of no use to them, whereas a larger church will need to be able to delegate work away from the PCC.

Preparation

The chair of a meeting bears the weight of responsibility to ensure that each time the group or committee meets the time spent together will be effective, fruitful and well used. In order for this to happen time spent in careful preparation will always be beneficial. This preparation will take a number of forms (and of course may be delegated to others, including the secretary, but it still remains the chair's responsibility).

Before reading further, a simple exercise would be for a less experienced chair (trainee) and a more experienced chair (trainer) to write down any preparation that needs to be undertaken before, say, the next PCC meeting, to compare notes and see then see how they compare.

Plan

In terms of overall preparation, there needs to be a plan as to frequency, timing, length and membership of meetings. It will be important to plan meetings in the context of other meetings and events taking place in a parish. So, for example, a PCC may meet every other month, alternating with the Standing Committee or perhaps nine times a year avoiding January, Easter and August. Meetings may be planned for 1½ or 2 hours (never longer) and at a regular slot so that everyone is clear and knows what they are committing to. Whatever is decided it should be clear and accessible, ideally with an annual programme.

Notice

Even with an annual programme good notice will need to be given in a way that is appropriate for the situation. In many parishes today this will include email, but it is important to take into account those who don't have diaries or who don't have access to email. Importantly, too, many people may have an email address but rarely actually access it. Simply sticking a notice on the notice board or in the service sheet is only useful if you *don't* want people to turn up!

Agenda

Who plans the agenda and how easy it is to have access to the agenda will be important decisions. In many parishes it will be the Standing Committee's job to plan the PCC agenda, but whatever the process, it needs to be transparent. Just because someone wants to put something on an agenda doesn't mean it has to go on, but a clear and transparent process will mean that it will be much easier to ensure that agenda decisions are justifiable and not personal. Agendas, together with other paperwork (see below), should be sent out in plenty of time for reading and assimilation (but not so much time that they get lost or forgotten!).

Putting approximate timings on an agenda can be very helpful as it gives people a feel of the priority being given to each item as well as helping the person chairing to keep control transparently. Also, agendas can be annotated in order to give a little more detail about an item, and perhaps include the name or initials of the person who has prime responsibility for the item. However, care should be given not to overload the detail on the agenda (which should never be more than two sides of A4 and better on one side).

Content

Agendas should be well balanced and varied and not repetitive, although formulaic agendas have their place, as people know what to expect. However, contrary to popular belief they do not have to start with approval of previous minutes and matters arising; so often this can lead to having the same meeting over and over again as matters arising can dominate the whole meeting. Turning the traditional meeting format on its head can be revolutionary. Common sense says that participants will be at their most fresh at the start of the meeting, so why not start with the most important item. At my last parish we developed a fairly standard format which can be found at the end of the chapter.

Paperwork

It will often be appropriate to have papers accompanying agendas giving details of an item and to set an expectation that people will have read such papers before a meeting. However, the presentation of such papers will need to vary enormously depending on participants. As a rule of thumb, though, the longer and/or denser the paper the less likely it is that people will have read it.

Any other business

Controlling AOB is a clear function of the chair. It will be crucial to have an unvarying policy on this. Meetings can so easily be ruined by a lone terrorist firing an Exocet missile in the closing stages of a meeting. The clear way to prevent this is to insist that AOB is offered to the chair either before or at the start of a meeting. It is then at the chair's discretion whether the item is discussed (briefly), referred to another committee or individual, placed on a future agenda or simply ruled as inappropriate. As chair you will be doing everybody else a huge favour by not submitting to inappropriate pressure.

The room

Perhaps one of the greatest influences on any meeting is the room. As a curate I used to complain of the amount of my time I would spend shifting chairs (they never had classes on chair shifting at my theological college!). However, after many years as a vicar I realize quite how important chair shifting is. It's all about preparing well for a meeting, group session, Bible study or worship. A well-prepared environment will include a correct temperature, appropriate seating well arranged, and a pleasant room. Preparing the room in advance can also (I believe) be a spiritual exercise in praying for the meeting, for those attending, and for your own contribution, and in placing the whole into God's hands.

The seating and layout will, though, also determine the nature of the meeting; sitting around in comfy chairs in the vicarage sitting room will help to set a very different agenda to hard-back chairs around a table in the church hall. It's not that one's right and the other wrong, just that one's relaxed and the other is businesslike and people will react accordingly. Similarly, if there is a top table for the chair and secretary (or churchwardens) with everyone else in a semicircle around, this will feel more like a classroom. Further, where the chair sits and who sits next to the chair will say something, whether intentionally or unintentionally.

Refreshments

Always a fraught issue. If AOB can ruin the end of a meeting, then refreshments can easily destroy the start of a meeting, with someone jumping up to make a cup of tea for each late arrival and making sure that everybody's had enough delicious cake. It is my firm opinion (though others will disagree) that refreshments take place in the 15 minutes before a meeting starts, and if you're late then you've missed them (or you help yourself). Refreshments half way through *never* take ten minutes and usually half an hour, and refreshments at the end make people feel guilty if they need to get home to see the family, and they encourage post-meeting cabals. However, sandwiches or snacks can be a life-saver for people who have dashed to a meeting directly from work.

Minutes

Does the meeting need to be formally minuted or would some short notes or action points be sufficient? Well, if it's the PCC then formal minutes will normally be important, but not necessarily so for other groups and committees. An informed decision will need to be made; there is clearly no need for reams of notes that nobody is ever going to read. The important issues will be to find someone to act as minute secretary who is both accurate and concise.

Minutes and notes should always be action orientated. This means that there should either be an *action by* column on the right-hand side and/or a summary of action points at the start of the minutes (ideally the latter can be emailed around straight after the meeting).

If a meeting is formally minuted, technically minutes are draft until they have been passed (with any amendments or corrections) at the next meeting. Occasionally people get very upset if minutes receive a wider circulation than the members before they have been approved. However, I always tend to go for maximum openness with meetings and (when I could get away with it) having a copy of the minutes put on the notice board at the back of church as soon as they were ready (nobody reads them, but it models transparency). A good practice, though, is to publish a very brief résumé in the Sunday notice sheet straight after the PCC meeting. Clearly, confidential or sensitive items need to be treated with great care.

Prayer

And finally, surround the whole event in prayer. Clearly praying at the beginning and end of every meeting will be important, but it will also be important for the chair to pray through the agenda before the meeting and pray for the people attending the meeting, by name. Holding up the business and the participants to God places the whole meeting in perspective. It may also be good to find people in the parish to pray for the meeting while it's taking place; this may be an invaluable ministry for someone who is housebound, for example.

Practicalities

So you've arrived and beautifully prepared the room, the agenda is prepared and the whole event is surrounded in prayer; you are clear about the need to develop the individuals and relationships and to keep the group on task; it should be a doddle. Of course, there are many possible pitfalls awaiting you, so here are some tips on practicalities which may help. First, though, think of a meeting that you've attended and write down the practical factors that have affected (for good or ill) the course of the meeting.

Welcome

It may seem a little over the top to be welcoming everyone individually as they arrive when you probably know them so well, but greeting each person can make a huge difference to the start of a meeting. It helps people feel that they have a part to play and that they have been noticed, and it also offers anyone who needs it an opportunity to get something off their chest, rather than carry it through the meeting.

Latecomers can be a nuisance, but it is usually best to welcome them and give them a very brief window to apologize. If they don't get this chance some may sit and stew for the whole meeting, particularly if they've just had a dreadful journey and really want you to know this. Their stewing can colour the meeting.

Pre-meetings should be avoided or ended well before the beginning of the main meeting. Walking into a room where a pre-meeting is in progress can be disconcerting and unwelcoming for participants. It can also give the perception that the pre-meeting is the *real* meeting and the main meeting has now been stitched-up.

Timing

It is crucial that meetings start and finish on time. If this is integrated into the culture of a church and is utterly consistent, then it will encourage people to arrive with an expectation of engagement from the beginning with a clear knowledge of what their commitment is and when they will be home by. If slippage creeps in, then people have a degree of uncertainty. Waiting for late-comers, over-running with refreshments or 'just finishing this item' soon makes people uncomfortable or irritated (though, of course, ending early seldom upsets anyone!).

Seating

Where people sit can't always be planned, but getting particular people to help in sitting by appropriate places can be useful. Having the vicar at the head of the table with a churchwarden on either side can, for example, say something about how the meeting is to progress; it *might* look like a stitch-up job. In one parish where I was vicar we had an individual who had lots to say about every item, much of which was incomprehensible; however, he saw himself as the elder statesman. My seating technique for him was to always sit next to him. First, this made him feel important, but from my point of view if I had sat opposite him it could easily have become confrontational. As it was, when I felt he'd had his say, I could turn to him and gently ask him to stop, sometimes placing my hand lightly on his arm. He was happy, because he felt he'd been heard; everyone else was happy, because he hadn't exploded and had been put back in his box; I was happy because I was (appropriately) in control in a non-confrontational way. Looking for ways to use seating well can really assist the flow of a meeting.

Introductions

Never assume that everyone knows everybody else (just because you do). This will be particularly important at the start of a new year (after the APCM, etc.), even if there is only one change. One change means that it is a new group and the dynamic will change accordingly, so everyone needs to be reintroduced in some way. Familiar ice-breaking techniques can be used here, even simple ones like asking each person to say what they best like about the church, etc. This will have the added benefit of ensuring that each person has spoken right at the beginning of the meeting, and has heard their own voice across the meeting (which will be particularly important for new members and for the less confident).

Introducing the meeting

After opening prayers and apologies for absence it is worth considering introducing the agenda – though only for a couple of minutes. This may include explaining the format for this particular meeting if it's different to others or indicating the priorities and explaining the amount of time allocated to particular items. It may be appropriate to remind participants of the context in which the meeting is taking place, the overall vision for the meeting, or recalling something of the shared values that the PCC have agreed. Doing this can help in ensuring that there is clarity and engagement among the participants.

Chairing the meeting

The participants should rely on the chair to keep a firm hand on the tiller during the meeting, while encouraging maximum participation. This is a tricky job, but vital if the meeting is to be both fruitful and effective. A check list of tips to help in keeping a meeting running smoothly can be found at the end of this chapter.

Progressing the meeting

Received wisdom seems to suggest that we sit down at the beginning of the meeting, address all our remarks through the chair and then get up at the end and leave. This can lead to a very boring experience and some uncomfortable bottoms. Further, it becomes very easy in this situation for a few strong voices to dominate the meeting. Don't be scared to:

- get people to buzz with their neighbours for a few minutes over a particular point – not only can this move a topic on, but it's an opportunity for the less vocal to have their say;
- divide up into small groups for a longer period, allowing a variety of opinions and options to be shared with the larger meeting;
- take short breaks, even if it's only two minutes for people to stand up and turn around, and particularly if debate has been heavy or controversial;
- ensure that there is water available for people to drink.

New ideas

Recognizing that different people have differing learning styles and preferences[1] will be important in attempting to keep everyone engaged in the process. For example, if a new idea is introduced an activist, if she likes it, will want to get on with it straightaway whereas a theorist will be keen to see the evidence and research supporting the idea; a pragmatist may want to hear of examples of other places where it has worked and a reflector will need some time to think about it. However, this may actually come across as a big fight on the issue if it's not handled sensitively.

A simple formula for new ideas might to use three meetings:

1. Introduce the idea at the end of the agenda, with no discussion but just giving notice, at one meeting.
2. Have the idea as the main agenda item at the second meeting, offering a variety of information to keep each of the learning preferences engaged.

---

1 www.businessballs.com/kolblearningstyles.htm or see Keith Lamdin and David Tilley, 2007, *Supporting New Ministers in the Local Church*, London: SPCK, p. 56f.

3. Make the decision at the third meeting, having allowed sufficient time for assimilation, exploration and discussion.

There is then something for everyone in the process (except, perhaps, your greatest fan who is also an activist, who just wants to get on with it!).

Parking

Every meeting will have someone who introduces irrelevancies, red herrings, distractions or complete misunderstandings. If the person is put down or ignored then not only will they feel belittled or angry, but others may well rush to support them (even though they don't agree with them). A very simple technique for dealing with such comments is to receive them and park them. The person then feels heard and the meeting can move on. A line such as 'thank you for that contribution, perhaps we may return to it later' or 'an interesting point, thank you' with full eye contact, can be very helpful; you may even write it down to show it has been received.

Awaydays

The use of awaydays can be very useful to help people to take a wider perspective. These should be well planned and away from home territory, in conducive surroundings. Strong consideration should be given to bringing in a skilled outside facilitator for the day. This will give space for someone else to ask the difficult questions and get behind the assumptions and givens that the group normally works with.

Social

Allow space to enjoy each other's company. An appropriate social activity every so often will allow people to meet together in a different way. However, do be careful that what is appropriate for one isn't alien or unnerving for another.

And finally

Do you have to chair every meeting yourself? If you have a good vice-chair, alternate meetings, and if you have the chair of a multinational in the congregation it might just be that she could do a better job (or at least advise you).

People

At the beginning of this chapter I spoke of the fact that at any meeting there are two things going on: the task or tasks to be fulfilled and the developing relationships, or to put it a different way, content and process. In chairing a meeting you will need to be an expert juggler as you will need not just to keep the meeting on task, but to be aware of the dynamic of the group and the needs of the individuals within that group.

Baggage

Everyone brings their own baggage into every situation. When arriving at a meeting, individuals might bring with them a bad day at work, the birth of a new grandchild, or a day spent at home without speaking to another person. Each of these will influence the way in which they engage with the meeting – and sometimes in quite profound ways. A normally mild- mannered person can suddenly explode across a meeting because of the appalling way he was treated at work that day. The outburst has nothing to do with the meeting, but he sees it as a 'safe' place. Similarly a normally totally engaged churchwarden is totally disengaged, because she can't wait to see her first grandchild the next day.

The baggage can, of course, go much deeper than this and bitterness, anger, joy or frustration from a lifetime shapes us as people, and all of this can be brought into a meeting. The image of two icebergs can be quite a useful one. We know that nine-tenths of an iceberg is below the waterline, so above the surface the two icebergs are a long way distant from each other, whereas below the surface they are crashing into one another. Very often the 'crashing' that takes place at a meeting is below the surface and can be about the previous hours, the previous Sunday or a furious row of five years ago.

Communications

Individuals' body language is a crucial indicator of the temperature of a meeting. It is really worth watching how people are reacting during a meeting. In communicating with others our body language – the way we sit, our mannerisms, our facial expressions – can give much away as to what we're really saying or how we're really feeling. Similarly, tone of voice can be more significant than the words used. We might use the most carefully selected phrases, but if our arms are folded, brow furrowed and tone of voice grumpy everyone knows what we're really saying!

Decisions

It is worth being aware of what people are really saying when they agree something in a meeting. There are multiple layers of 'yes' and 'no'! A simple test is to ask yourself whether a 'yes' is acquiescence (it doesn't affect or bother me), agreement (that's fine as long as I don't have to do anything about it) or ownership (I'm up for this and I'm willing to be a part of it). In my experience most people in meetings most of the time are hovering somewhere between acquiescence and agreement. What will they say when they bump into someone else from church who disagrees with the decision? The real challenge of chairmanship is to get ownership.

Priorities

A hard lesson I learned as a vicar was that the priorities of the members of the PCC would never match my priorities. However much I might talk of mission, evangelism and the good news of Jesus Christ, the reality was that the prime focus of my working life was the life, work and mission of the church in that place. Every other member of the PCC had jobs to keep down, mortgages or rent to pay, families to care for, and a thousand and one other concerns. The work of the PCC and therefore the mission of the church was never going to have the same priority for them as it was for me – simply because of the hours I had to devote to this. That is nothing to do with where they saw God in their lives, their spiritual lives, their fervour and life in the Spirit. It is simply a practical issue.

Recognizing and naming this is actually liberating as it reduces levels of guilt, brings expectations to a more reasonable level, and helps to value each person's contribution. It can also provide an opportunity to recognize (and rejoice in) the diversity of people's lives and the rounded experience and wisdom that each brings to the situation.

Last word

Chairing effective and fruitful meetings, then, can seem a huge mountain to climb, but always remember that it is not meant to be a solitary job. I have already suggested consideration be made of not chairing every meeting yourself. But further, in any meeting there will be people very much on your side with ample skills, experience and wisdom to support you. Use them. Ask others to watch out for issues that are revealing themselves; whether it's watching for body language or simply looking for support over a particular issue, ensure people will come to your aid – or even disagree with you in a friendly and helpful way.

I reckon that losing my first argument in a PCC was in a sense a victory, because it meant that the PCC trusted me, as vicar, enough to disagree with me (even though I didn't appreciate it at the time!).

And finally, it is God's church, not yours and not the PCC's. God finds a way of using every situation for good if we give God the space to do so. However the meeting went, into your hands, O Lord, I commit it.

Recommended reading

James Behrens, 2005, *Practical Church Management*, Leominster: Gracewing.

Church Representation Rules, 2011, London: Church House Publishing.

Martin Dudley and Virginia Rounding, 2008, *Churchwardens: A Survival Guide*, London: SPCK.

Martin Dudley and Virginia Rounding, 2009, *The Parish Survival Guide*, London: SPCK.

Kenneth Macmorran and Timothy Briden, 2010, *Handbook for Churchwardens and Parochial Church Councillors*, London: Continuum.

David Parrott, 2011, *Your Church and the Law*, Norwich: Canterbury Press.

John Pitchford, 2008, *An ABC for the PCC*, London: Continuum.

Ian Smith, 2006, *The Good Parish Management Guide*, Norwich: Canterbury Press.

Committee structure

The Standing Committee. This is the only statutory committee after the PCC and will normally include the incumbent, churchwardens, PCC secretary and often the treasurer. There may be one or two other members. Its principal function is to transact urgent business between PCC meetings and it will usually have delegated authority from the PCC.

Subcommittees. These can include Finance, Fabric, Mission, Social, Stewardship, Worship, etc. There is no set structure and each PCC will need to agree what is appropriate for their situation (ensuring that the structure is liberating and not burdensome). Subcommittees will have delegated authority, negotiated from the PCC, and will report to the PCC. They will also have a budget and an agreed limit that they can spend without reference to the PCC.

Working Groups. Examples will include Fundraising, Redevelopment, Strategy and Planning, etc. These will be time limited to carry out a particular task. Their delegated authority is likely to be less than that of a subcommittee and again they will report to the PCC.

Ministry Leadership Team, Staff Meeting. Such groups will normally be concerned with the day-to-day business of parish life, including pastoral concerns, worship and other ministry issues. They will interpret and enact the policies and vision set by the PCC.

An alternative PCC agenda

1. Apologies for absence
2. Bible study (20 minutes)
3. Main item (40 minutes)
4. Break (5 minutes)
5. Finance (15 minutes)
6. Other item (10 minutes)
7. Other item (10 minutes)
8. Minutes of the last meeting (5 minutes)
9. Matters arising (10 minutes)
10. Any other urgent business (5 minutes)

Incorporating a Bible study into the beginning of the agenda grounded us, reminding us of the context of the meeting. (It was a parish which wasn't very used to regular Bible study groups, so it also modelled good practice. We generally looked at the Gospel for the following Sunday, which also meant that the PCC members were more engaged with the sermon – and put the preacher on his or her mettle!) In the parish where I served as curate PCC meetings were always preceded by a Eucharist in church; the problem with this was that people saw it as an optional extra, however it was promoted. Integrating the Bible study within the meeting doesn't give this opportunity.

Some top tips for chairing a meeting

An effective chair will

- keep to the agenda and the business in hand;
- keep a check on red herrings and diversions;
- ensure clarity of responsibility for decisions made;
- encourage quiet members and keep noisy ones in check;
- not do all the speaking herself/himself;
- give space for the assimilation of new ideas;
- keep the meeting interesting and lively;
- not allow the same items to keep recurring unless there is good reason and forward motion;
- keep hobby-horses in check (including their own!);
- ensure that everyone is clear about what is going on during the meeting (this may include encouraging 'stupid' questions – these are often the ones that everyone is dying to ask, but too embarrassed!);
- clarify points where necessary, and ask others for clarification;
- listen attentively to those speaking, modelling good practice;
- protect the rights of others to have their own opinions or thoughts heard;
- allow disagreement and constructive debate;
- challenge inappropriate comments, opinions or behaviour (racism, sexism, rudeness, etc.);
- make use of the skills and wisdom of others;
- summarize and ensure that people agree with the summary.

The chair is the co-ordinator and enabler of a meeting, not the dictator, the fount of all wisdom and knowledge, nor master of all skills.

13

Continuing Professional Development

TIM LING

We come to God not by navigation but by eternal love. (Augustine of Hippo)

This book encourages the development of faithful ministers. Each chapter draws attention to a dimension of the training relationship or to practical skills in ministry, roles and tasks that may be performed with varying degrees of proficiency. We advocate the value in certain patterns of behaviour, occasionally making reference to the desirability of managing risk. As a whole the book asserts that developing ministry is an activity that demands serious attention. However, in doing so there is a palpable discomfort, a wrestling with the possibility that our understandings of vocation and faithfulness may not cohere with institutional realities and language. In this chapter I explore why this is such a pressing and challenging issue, and reflect on how engaging in continuing 'professional' development is inextricably linked with faithful ministry.

Why is ministry development such a pressing issue?

I believe that three interrelated themes particularly crowd our attention when considering ministerial development, particularly for the Church of England's clergy.[1] These are legislation, managerialism and role confusion. There is also a fourth important and sometimes eclipsed consideration: God's mission.

Legislation

The Church of England has developed a new form of 'common tenure' for its clergy: *The Ecclesiastical Offices (Terms of Service) Measure 2009.*[2]

---

1 While this chapter focuses on clergy I believe the themes and issues relate to all forms of licensed ministry.

2 For a full discussion of rationale, see: *Review of Clergy Terms of Service: Part Two Report on the second phase of the work*, GS 1564 (Church of England, 2005).

This was partly in response to Section 23 of the Employment Relations Act 1999, which gave the UK government power to explicitly include categories of workers within the scope of employment protection legislation, such as religious office holders. These new 'Terms of Service' have sought therefore to ensure good practice within a broader context of professional human resources management providing: clear terms and conditions of service, ministerial development review, continuing ministerial education and development, and transparent capability and grievance procedures.

Managerialism

This is the belief that organizations are sufficiently similar in their underlying make-up for their performance to be optimized by the application of generic management skills and theory. When the Archbishop of Canterbury talks in terms of 'vision', 'growth', 'effectiveness' and 'strategic resource allocation' as he did in his presidential address to the new General Synod in November 2010, the reality of this prevailing discourse is clear. You cannot ignore the sound of epistemic cultures clashing as you place measurement, audit and accountability alongside professional autonomy, community and folly for Christ's sake (1 Cor. 3.18).[3]

Role confusion

The clergy's identity in the context of late modernity is characterized by ambiguity and uncertainty. A role that could once be located at the centre of society now finds both an absence of society and an experience of marginalization.[4] This has been accompanied by increasing demands, particularly with the growth of ministry across multiple parishes and expectations that ministry should be shared, i.e. 'collaborative'.[5] The solo pastoral ministry lived within a particular community is a feature of a bygone era and now rarely possible.[6] This is not something that is widely understood by society. Clergy are not alone in experiencing this loss and like other

---

3 This is particularly evident in the recent contributions to a special edition of the journal *Studies in Christian Ethics* (Vol. 21, No. 1, 2008) dedicated to the topic of 'Managerialism in the Church'.

4 John Williams, 2011, '21st Century Shapes of the Church to come?', *Theology*, Vol. 114, No. 2, pp. 108–19.

5 Robin Greenwood, 2009, *Parish Priests: For the sake of the Kingdom*, London: SPCK.

6 Ronny Lamont, 2011, *Leaping the Vicarage Wall: Leaving Parish Ministry*, London: Continuum.

professions they are striving to come to terms with their contested vocational identities.[7]

However, while these themes demand our attention I believe that they should not obscure the more fundamental reason for attending to ministry development, that is, as a response to God's ongoing call. God calls men and women in his service 'to go and bear fruit, fruit that will last' (John 15.16). We keep ourselves from being 'ineffective and unproductive' in our response to this call not through the exercise of technical competence but through growing in personal qualities: faithfulness, goodness, knowledge, self-control, perseverance, godliness, kindness and love (cf. 2 Peter 1.5–7). 'Effective ministerial presence is essential if people are to be in touch with the faithfulness of God through the Church.'[8] It is because we truly care about God's mission that we take care in our practice. In encouraging the development of effective ministry this desire is essentially rooted in a call to respond to God's faithfulness.

'Great rhetoric', you might say, 'but what about reality?' The practical theologian van der Ven suggests that our dominant responses have fallen into one of three categories: attempts to construct a new, more easily defended order; naïve hope that there will be a return to halcyon days; and denial.[9] The apposite nature of this thesis is evident in the Archbishop of Canterbury's address to the July 2011 Synod where he tackled his critics by asserting that 'we are never likely to return to the mythical past' with a resident full-time pastor in every small parish, and questioned whether we have 'yielded too much to the pressure of university accreditation'. I believe there is an alternative to these false hopes and attempts to restore status through credentialism. Indeed, that it involves a faithfulness that lies at the heart of ministry.

In order to help us to explore our present condition further and how it may relate to the possibility of developing faithful ministers I am going to reflect on what it might mean to be a 'professional'.

Professional ministry

As a professional the minister has an individual and institutional role and responsibility. (GS Misc. 122)

---

7 B. Wilson, 2001, 'Salvation, Secularisation, and De-moralisation', in E. Fenn (ed.), *Sociology of Religion*, Oxford: Blackwell.

8 Rowan Williams, 2011, http://www.archbishopofcanterbury.org/articles.php/2122/archbishop-of-canterburys-presidential-address (accessed 7th November 2011).

9 J. A. van der Ven, 1998, *Education for Reflective Ministry*, Leuven: Peeters Press.

In common usage a professional is a member of an occupation that requires specialized knowledge and skills to practise and in whom one can place one's trust at least in respect of this area of practice. Yet the idea that a minister might be a professional often meets a troubling reception. Indeed, the Baptist theologian John Piper, writing from a North American perspective, says: 'We Pastors *are being killed* by the professionalising of the pastoral ministry.'[10] Why the discomfort? Is there some special virtue in isolated, ignorant and incompetent practice? Or does the discomfort lie elsewhere? Moving beyond John Piper's rhetoric, it appears that his concern lies with the danger of misplaced desires, particularly around lifestyle and status.[11] The Church of England's report GS Misc. 122 *The Continuing Education of the Church's Ministers* owns this discomfort and explicitly states that its use of the label is not about ascribing status but describing 'a distinctive style of activity'. This style of activity finds roots, as does our language, in the tenth century in the context of monasticism: the professional is someone who makes a public profession and enters a disciplined community. The sociologist Max Weber, who famously identified monks as the first professionals, uses the word *Beruf* 'profession', which may also be translated 'calling', to draw attention to what he believed to be the first rational human beings, working methodically, towards a common goal – a future life.[12] A serious consequence of this 'distinctive style of activity' which can be observed time and again through history is that the professionals' success has led to the accrual of wealth, status and power, and correspondingly laxity, corruption and decline.[13] Our discomfort with the language has partly reflected this underlying association with power. However, I believe that there is another more contemporary and perhaps more disturbing dimension to our discomfort: the professional's loss of status with the emergence of a technocratic 'skills society'.

The 'skills society' and the 'job'

However, the professional advice of those who analysed the results was that the job satisfaction figures for clergy were substantially higher than for the population at large. (GS 1408)

---

10 J. Piper, 2003, *Brothers we are not Professionals: A Plea to Pastors for Radical Ministry*, Fearn: Mentor.

11 See David Heywood, 2011, *Reimagining Ministry*, London: SCM Press, pp. 2–9 for his overview of the emergence of professional ministry and its relation to status preservation.

12 'Only for him did the clock strike, only for him were the hours of the day divided – for prayer.' Max Weber, 1981, *General Economic History*, Transaction Publishers, p. 365.

13 M. Hill, 1973, *The Religious Order: A Study of Virtuoso Religion and its Legitimation in the Nineteenth-century Church of England*, London: Heinemann.

When I first read the above, which reflects on the responses from over six thousand clergy, the thing that surprised me was not the result but the language – 'job satisfaction'. I consciously avoid talking about ministry in terms of a 'job'. Instinctively I react against this language which I feel runs counter to understandings of a professional's autonomy and the priest's office-holder status. Richard Sennett draws attention to the word's root in old English as a 'lump of coal' or a 'pile of wood' that could be moved around at will.[14] He goes on to discuss the emergence of our contemporary 'skills society' where jobs, in this old sense of random movement, now prevail and create a sense of work life as little more than a series of disconnected events. The professional's mystique, built up through the delivery of specialized services based on exceptional knowledge, has been unmasked by the very technical rationality that gave them power. I can now buy a 'will kit' at the supermarket, self-diagnose online, and cut and paste a wedding liturgy via the Church of England website. This democratization of knowledge has facilitated a sceptical reassessment of the professions' actual contribution to society's well-being.[15]

In this 'skills society' there has been a steady erosion of the professional's status. There has been a proliferation of 'professions' accompanied by the prescription of progressively more detailed criteria for the performance of a succession of 'jobs'. In parallel with these moves the public have frequently found the professional wanting or their services simply mundane. This trend is beautifully satirized in the film *The Incredibles*, a cartoon fable about a family of superheroes' lost and rediscovered vocation. In a legislative and risk-averse climate the 'Supers' have fallen out of favour with the public. There is a scene where Mr Incredible has been captured by his nemesis Syndrome. Syndrome is not a 'Super' but has super powers by virtue of technological innovations. He explains with glee to Mr Incredible that when he retires he will sell all these innovations: 'And when everyone becomes super, no-one will be super.' When everyone becomes a professional, no-one will be professional? This being Hollywood there is a happy ending. Syndrome overreaches himself. He never gets to retire. The public rediscover the value of the superheroes and the Incredibles rediscover their vocation. We do not live in 'Hollywood'. We live in the midst of this cultural change, which has also seen the loss of the career.

14 R. Sennett, 2008, *The Craftsman*, London: Allen Lane, p. 265.
15 D. Schön, 1991, *The Reflective Practitioner: How Professionals Think in Action*, Aldershot: Ashgate, p. 13.

The career

There was this idea in the past where getting to the Times was almost like getting tenure and you'd have this great thirty to forty year career where you'd cover politics, you'd cover some foreign, and maybe write a book and that's not the track now. (Tim Arango, Corporate Media Reporter, *The New York Times*)[16]

When Tim Arango reflects 'that's not the track now', he is echoing the root meaning of career. In old English a career meant 'a well-laid road'. He is also more broadly echoing the refrain sometimes heard from clergy: 'This isn't the Church I was ordained into.'[17] There was a time when a priest ordained in the Church of England followed a clear path. It started with a young man who advanced through first and second curacies to getting a small parish 'of their own' or joining a team ministry, followed by a larger more desirable parish,[18] a curate, diocesan responsibilities, and closed with the invitation to become an honorary canon. This 'well-laid road' is now a road less travelled. We are in a profoundly different place marked by different 'styles of church life',[19] models of ministry and institutional realities. We live in a 'mixed economy' where our understanding of church life, its maintenance and its relation to God's mission are still developing. John Williams in a recent article for *Theology* has talked about twenty-first-century 'shapes of church' and set out as many as six: Retrieving the Tradition, Local Ministry, Mission Shaped Church, Fresh Expressions, Post-Christendom, and Emergent Churches.[20] These 'shapes' or 'styles' have generated both champions and reading lists. They have also contributed to different emphases in the understanding of ministry: the pastor, the collaborator, the leader, the pioneer, the navigator etc. In this context the Church of England's Archbishops' Council has as a priority 'to re-shape or reimagine the Church's ministry for the century coming'.[21] The institutional backdrop to these changes has included a shift from stipendiary to self-supporting ministry, residential to non-residential,

---

16 BBC4 *Storyville – Deadline*: The New York Times, http://www.bbc.co.uk/iplayer/episode/b017j25x/Storyville_20112012_Deadline_The_New_York_Times/ (accessed 11th December 2011).

17 See further 'Not the Church I was ordained in – Alleluiah', *Church Times*, 8th July 2011.

18 Lamont, *Leaping*, p. 84.

19 RowanWilliams, 2003, http://www.archbishopofcanterbury.org/articles.php/1826/archbishops-presidential-address-general-synod-york-july-2003 (accessed 27th December 2011).

20 J. Williams, 'Shapes of the Church'.

21 GS 1815.

male to female, young to old.[22] One result is a more rapid and demanding transition into a complex incumbency, another is the rise in the number of dual-clergy households that means: 'chaplaincy can be a career choice that enables two ordained clergy to each receive pay for their work'.[23] Chaplaincy or minister-in-secular employment, paid or unpaid, 'full-time' or 'part-time', deployable or local, parochial or pioneer, are 'career choices' that may be liberating but may also be profoundly disturbing to well-laid roads, whether real or imagined. This is not simply an issue for clergy. The academic literature on the professions discusses the emergence of 'boundaryless careers' which place the onus on the individual to take responsibility for their management.[24] Unless the individual takes responsibility, there is a real danger in this less paternalistic environment that they find themselves at the mercy of a myriad of competing voices expecting them to simply perform a succession of 'jobs'. This is implicitly recognized in the new 'common tenure' for Church of England clergy and its advocacy for role descriptions as a means of managing unrealistic expectations. How might this relate to our understanding of calling?

Calling

Is the life I am living the same as the life that wants to live in me?
(Parker J. Palmer)

In discussing jobs and careers I have intended to draw attention to what may underlie some of our discomfort with the attribution of the label 'professional'. I have suggested that the discomfort may be attributed to how we live with both the accrual and the loss of worldly security and status. Indeed, our feeling a sense of discomfort may be a healthy state. Painting with very broad brush strokes, over that last 50 years, the clerical response to what appeared to be society's secularization by attempting to 'shore up their claims to status' through the professionalization of ministry, and the more contemporary disassociation with such initiatives, highlight how

---

22 Martyn Percy, 2010, *Shaping the Church: The Promise of Implicit Theology*, Farnham: Ashgate, p. 132. 'Here at Cuddesdon, the average age of ordinands currently in residential training is 38, and those in non-residential training 49. The male–female ratio is 50:50.' Cf. the official Church of England statistics: http://www.churchofengland.org/media/1333106/2009churchstatistics.pdf (accessed 7th November 2011).

23 Miranda Threlfall-Holmes and Mark Newitt, 2011, *Being a Chaplain*, London: SPCK.

24 J. Sturges et al., 2005, 'Managing the career deal: The psychological contract as a framework for understanding career management, organizational commitment and work behavior', *Journal of Organizational Behavior* 26, pp. 821–38.

the Church and its ministers are necessarily and inextricably caught up in the world.[25] It also draws attention to misdirected or excessive desires, particularly the desire for control and the denial of dependence, our sinfulness, and our need for salvation. We live in a broken world, and God calls us not out of this world but to become God's people in the world. Our profession, our *Beruf*, our calling, is not simply a task or a role. A calling inseparably links identity and occupation; all work is imbued with meaning and value. It is about living out our blessings in Christ, about receiving a gift not achieving a goal.

The word 'ministry' in its broadest sense denotes the service to which the whole people of God are called. While all are called, there is a special responsibility placed upon those in licensed ministry. In order to engage with and fulfil God's mission, the Church needs men and women who are 'publicly and continually responsible for pointing to its fundamental dependence on Jesus Christ'.[26] This cannot be reduced to roles and tasks. The discourse neatly set out by Martyn Percy in *Clergy: The Origin of Species*, which sees the work clergy 'entered ministry for – serving, helping, relating, preaching and liturgical' – as being 'increasingly squeezed out by other demands', is troubling. When I hear the refrain 'I wasn't called to . . .', which typically ends with a task such as 'arrange for a contractor to fix the church heating', I am filled both with compassion and an uneasiness.[27] Uneasiness, because it echoes the narratives of many members of Generations X and Y who have been formed in a culture of choice and consumption, as Berg et al. have put it they have 'internalised the idealistic belief that they can become anything they want or dream to be', and, 'expect that they will be able to answer these callings'.[28] This often results in heroic behaviour that literally involves self-sacrifice.[29] However, in the outworking of these grand visions there appears to be little appreciation that a calling might be 'neither challenging nor enjoyable [while] a career may be both'.[30] It is telling that Martyn Percy talks of some clergy 'leaving

25 B. Wilson, 1969, 'Major Patterns of Religion', in R. Robertson (ed.), *Sociology of Religion*, Harrmondsworth: Penguin, p. 154 and A. Roxburgh, *The Missionary Congregation, Leadership and Liminality*, Harrisburg: Trinity Press, pp. 43f.

26 World Council of Churches, 1982, *Baptism, Eucharist and Ministry*, Faith and Order Paper No. 111, Geneva: World Council of Churches.

27 Martyn Percy, 2006, *Clergy: The Origin of Species*, London: Continuum, p. 163.

28 Grant Berg and Johnson, 2010, 'Unanswered Occupational Callings', *Organisational Science* 21(5), p. 975.

29 P. J. Palmer, 2000, *Let your Life Speak: Listening for the Voice of Vocation*, San Francisco: Jossey-Bass, p. 4: 'Trying to live someone else's life or to live by an abstracted norm, will inevitably fail – and may even do great damage.'

30 A. Wrzesniewski et al., 1997, 'Jobs, Careers and Callings: People's Relations to their Work', *Journal of Research in Personality* 31, p. 23.

ministry to find "more definite" careers'. Public ministry is not about the exercise of a charism for personal fulfilment. The vocation of the minister is inextricably bound up with the vocation of the Church through which that ministry is exercised. For many the Church and the gospel are what the minister is.[31] Whatever their personal abilities or attractiveness, these cannot release the minister from taking public responsibility for the Church. Equally their public role will not wholly obscure any personal deficiencies they may have.[32] In God's economy, how one goes about fixing the heating matters.

Gift

As a steward of God's mysteries, the priest is a special witness to the Invisible in the world. For he is a steward of invisible and priceless treasures belonging to the spiritual and supernatural order. (Pope John Paul II[33])

The preceding discussion has touched on some major theological themes: God's grace, our humanity and Jesus' faithfulness. When I think of an individual's gifts, I want to attribute these to God as creator and provider of all good things (Rom. 8.28). Responding to God's ongoing call involves an acknowledgement of God as gracious giver and source of all goodness. However, such facts do not set aside the reality of our humanity, of secular authorities, and the darkness within us that makes us dangerous and dissatisfied.[34] Nonetheless, when we struggle with both conscious and unconscious demands, our desire to assert status, our lust to dominate, our pride and denial of dependence, we may start to own our belongingness to God. When I think of jobs and the career as a 'well-laid path', I am led to think of Jesus as 'the way' (John 14.6) and the challenge to 'follow in his steps' (1 Peter 2.21). These steps do not take us out of the world but take the form of a faithful obedience to the Father, living a mortal life 'to the point of death' (Phil. 2.8), in the world. What we are being asked for is a total commitment, to give up our lives.

31 Cf. Paul Bayes' reflections in this volume on the findings of the Church of England's 'Weddings Project' and the importance of the role of the 'vicar'.
32 GS Misc. 122 p. 9.
33 Pope John Paul II, 1997, *Gift and Mystery*, London: Doubleday, p. 87.
34 Rod Garner, 2011, *On Being Saved: The Roots of Redemption*, London: Darton, Longman and Todd, p. 25.

The deep sense of personal fulfilment that the prevailing culture encourages individuals to expect from their work often runs counter to the structures and practices that the organizations they work for deem practical for achieving their goals. Cultural norms drive us to pursue such 'callings', employment systems may provide limited opportunities. We wrestle with the possibility that our understandings of vocation and faithfulness may not cohere with institutional realities, and language is not simply a challenge for the Church. Indeed, how people craft work and leisure time in pursuit of unanswered occupational callings is the subject of academic study.[35] When people recognize that their work situations are misaligned with their personal values, needs and preferences, and the situation allows for a degree of autonomy, they engage in strategies of 'task emphasising', 'job expanding' and 'role reframing' in order to find meaning.[36] When they work in less permissive situations they seek out in their leisure time 'vicarious experiences' and 'hobby participation' in activities aligned to their sense of calling.[37] These various strategies result in positive feelings of enjoyment and meaning. They can also lead to regret over forgone fulfillment and increased stress and overload due to the difficulties involved in such crafting activity. I suspect that this is a contributory factor in some clergy burnout.

This is an issue that is particularly felt by the artist,[38] who often seeks to maintain boundaries between their art, frequently conceived of as a gift, and commerce, which is understood to have the potential to destroy, or 'collapse' the intuitive impulse. Lewis Hyde has identified three pathways adopted by artists. Some find second jobs, and others find patrons to support them. These first two routes are about creating a structural means to mark out a boundary between their art and the market. The third way is to place the work itself on the market generating fees and royalties. This latter category, the artist who sells his own creations, must develop a more subjective feel for the two economies of gift and commerce – to work on a boundaryless path? Hyde writes:

He must, on the one hand be able to disengage from the work and think of it as a commodity. He must be able to reckon its value in terms of current fashions, know what the market will bear, demand fair value, and part with the work when someone pays the price. And he must, on the other hand, be able to forget all that and turn to serve his own gifts

35 Berg and Johnson, 'Unanswered Occupational Callings'.
36 Berg and Johnson, 'Unanswered Occupational Callings', pp. 978f.
37 Berg and Johnson, 'Unanswered Occupational Callings', pp. 982f.
38 Schön, *Reflective Practitioner*, p. 18.

on their own terms. If he cannot do the former, he cannot hope to sell his art, and if he cannot do the latter, he may have no art to sell, or only commercial art, work that has been created in response to the market, not in response to the demands of the gift.[39]

The setting up of boundaries, the crafting of our work, to serve the demands of our gift does not sit well with an understanding of vocation that is about integration of life and work rather than fragmentation. In the Church of England ministers have historically been in receipt of a stipend, a form of patronage that has granted them the freedom to exercise their gift.[40] At least in theory this has released them from being a chaplain to a congregation in order to act as a priest to the whole parish. Now with changes in demographics, in tenure and in the financial demands placed on parishes ministers are being asked to be much more accountable, to take the boundaryless path and to develop a capacity to bring their gift to the market. There is a real fear that this represents a loss of freedom to function creatively. Paradoxically it calls for greater creativity and integration of vocation. This is not simply an issue for those in receipt of a stipend. The non-stipendiary or self-supporting minister is in receipt of an income from a 'second job', either a pension or paid employment, or supported through patronage, from family or spouse. These are not unambiguous relationships and require attention. Within each of Hyde's paths it is necessary to attend to how boundaries are managed and the demands of the 'gift' are served. To what extent does our stewardship (or crafting) of our calling contribute to integrated or disintegrated lives?

Professional development

We see then that the two cities were created by two kinds of love: the earthly city was created by self-love reaching the point of contempt for God, the Heavenly City by the love of God carried as far as contempt for the self. (Augustine of Hippo, *De civ.* XVI, 28)

The idea that our wrestling with professional or ministerial identities is a particular challenge for this age is a false notion. Peter challenges us to

---

39 Lewis Hyde, 2006, *The Gift: How the Creative Spirit Transforms the World*, Edinburgh: Canongate, p. 279.

40 See Lee Longdon's 2011 DThM thesis: *Mission-Shaped Curacy? Reshaping Curacy for Effective Formation for Authentic Ministry in the 21st Century Church of England*, Birmingham University, pp.101f.

follow Jesus' example of faithfulness and to explore the meaning of our status as resident aliens (1 Peter 2.11–12). These are themes that Augustine works on at length in his *City of God*, a book about being other-worldly in the world.[41] In the tenth century our 'first professionals', the religious orders, aimed to radically live out the ideal values of their society whilst at the same time offering a living critique of that society. Their restatement of that which they profess, along with their disciplined and prophetic life together, were faithful responses to God's bountiful grace and a model for others. The early Methodists and the Oxford Movement transformed themselves, and the society around them, through the rigorous restatement of existing traditions combined with disciplined and active lives.[42] For these 'professionals' there was no denial of the messy realities of daily life or flight to more easily defended identities. Rather their charge was to accept dependence upon God in daily life and to live faithfully not for worldly status but for the world. The continuing professional development that this book advocates stands in this tradition. Its common themes have been well laid through the centuries. First, that this is God's business. Our development is rooted in God's trusting and entrusting, his creativity and confidence, his faithfulness and timing. Second, that God is interested in our present realities, the 'rich eccentricity of human lives'. Our joys and triumphs, our mistakes and vulgarity, are all moments when we may seriously encounter and share in the Holy Spirit's work. Third, because our development is rooted both in God's faithfulness and our humanity we should continually practise wisdom:

1. Intentionally, stating clearly what we value: remembering, not only through seasons, symbols and stories, but also through learning agreements, the law, and even, checklists; and, refining, through prayer, critical conversations and questioning. Because we have a calling our jobs matter.
2. In company, the Church is essentially a pilgrim community. God is calling us into relationship with him and each other. We learn together by practising what we value with each other, 'hanging out with old-timers', making friends, and giving and receiving feedback. Because we have a calling our career matters.
3. Expectantly, prepared and preparing to be transformed, waiting for a God 'whose providence and purpose unfolds in his time'. Our

---

41 For the uninitiated, Peter Brown, 1967, *Augustine of Hippo*, London, Faber and Faber, pp. 313–29 is a good place to start.
42 Hill, *Religious Order*.

development depends on willingness 'to lose the argument', vulnerability, and openness to the possibility of something new. This work is prophetic.

The lessons of this book may help you to navigate the competing expectations and performance demands of a changing world. They may also help you to execute a succession of jobs with confidence. However, my hope is that they will prepare you first and foremost for faithful pilgrimage and to grow in that which we profess, God's love. It is the task for those of us involved in ministerial development to help to create spaces for this to happen. In all our activity may we be shaping communities that help us to see the world as it really is, through the medium of God's love.

Further reading

Church of England General Synod, *Challenges for the New Quinquennium: A report from the House of Bishops and the Archbishops' Council*, GS 1815, London: General Synod. Available at www.churchofengland.org/media/1163101/gs%201815.pdf.

Church of England General Synod, 2001, *Generosity and Sacrifice: The report of the Clergy Stipends Review Group*, GS 1418, London: Church House Publishing.

Church of England General Synod, 1980, *The Continuing Education of the Church's Ministers*, GS Misc. 122 London: ACCM, 1980.

Rowan Williams, 2010, http://www.archbishopofcanterbury.org/articles.php/919/archbishops-presidential-address-general-synod-november-2010 (accessed 7th November 2011).

Appendix

Learning Outcomes Exercises

LESLEY BENTLEY

The House of Bishops' Learning Outcomes are unlike those found more commonly in education in referring to such elements as character, relationships and spirituality, rather than simply demonstrable skills. They are intended to give guidance to the curate and the wider Church about what is looked for in an effective minster. Sue Cross on page 56 of her chapter in this book welcomes the learning outcomes 'for what they are: a tool, albeit imperfect . . . designed to help us to do a difficult job better'. She goes on to describe how the learning outcomes can be used to enhance learning and avoiding a 'tick-box mentality'. The exercises below suggest some ways in which the chapters of this book might be used to enable those in IME 4–7 to work with the Learning Outcomes. Stuart Burns in his chapter warns against the Learning Outcomes being used in a way that makes it appear that learning can stop at the end of curacy, when it may appear that agreement has been reached that the outcomes have been met.

Part 1 Faithfulness

Confidence in calling

Related Learning Outcomes: Vocation, Spirituality and Quality of Mind

At the completion of IME curates are expected to 'be able to give an account of their vocation to ministry and mission and their readiness to receive and exercise ordained ministry as a priest within the Church of God'. Write a reflection on how your understanding of your calling has developed since you were ordained deacon. What have you learned particularly in the 'swampy areas'? Have there been occasions where you were particularly conscious of your calling as part of the calling of the Church rather than just you as an individual? Can you describe how your trust and dependence upon God have increased? Has your commitment or vocation been threatened at any point and if so, where has this taken you? If God is the sower, how would you now describe the condition of the seed?

Making friends

Related Learning Outcomes: Spirituality, Personality and Character, Relationships

This chapter presents a tension between the role of priest and living as a friend and in community within the parish(es). This tension underlies the Learning Outcomes listed above.

Reflecting on your life and ministry in your parish,

- In what ways do you consider you demonstrate loving service? (Spirituality) What are the areas of your life and ministry that you need to work on?
- Where do your relationships demonstrate that you are a member of a community of friends? Which relationships require some prayerful attention?
- Could you use the description of an 'open, defenceless, fully "given" pastoral leader of yourself'? What would you need to change in your parochial relationships to do this? Would you then consider this to be an appropriate way to behave in your role?

Priestly formation

Related Learning Outcomes: Vocation, Spirituality

The Learning Outcomes concern themselves primarily with formation in ministry rather than skills. Formation is harder to describe and even harder to quantify – yet the Church wants to know that its priests are people being shaped in the image of Christ, 'rooted and growing in a life of prayer' and 'sustained and energized by trust in and dependence on the gifting and grace of God'.

Using the four headings of Andrew Mayes' chapter, spend some time in reflection upon how you have been formed, since you were ordained by Word, Worship, Woundedness and Wonder. Share your thinking with your spiritual director or soul friend.

Part 2 – Development

Teacher–learner relationship

Related Learning Outcomes: Faith, Quality of Mind and Vocation

Take time to consider. Where are the spaces in your ministry for deliberate reflection? A journal may be an appropriate way of giving you space for reflection, as may regular quiet days and periodic retreats. Reflection should be in depth on aspects of your ministry and pastoral situations that you encounter. It should also concern the breadth of your ministerial experience. Are you getting the variety of experience that will enable you to prepare for the next stage of your ministry? The Learning Outcomes can be helpful here, in indicating areas of experience that are lacking.

Who are your teachers in the parish? Are there others from whom you could set out to learn?

How deeply are you taking the theological reflection in your supervision sessions? If the answer is that this is not deep, could you agree ways of deepening the reflection with your incumbent, perhaps by sharing the reading of a book or presenting your thinking in a more formal way to your incumbent or other staff?

Asking questions

Related Learning Outcomes: Mission and Evangelism, Leadership and Collaboration, Personality and Character, Relationships, Faith

Within this chapter there are a number of questions already offered. The questions could be particularly useful within supervision. Try these questions and share with your training minister. They are arranged in the order in which they appear in the chapter. The Learning Outcomes to which they relate are given in brackets at the end of each question.

1. What questions could you make use of with the people you want to see grow in faith and commitment? (Mission and Evangelism)
2. How might this (openness and vulnerability and a willingness to listen to those less experienced or with less authority in the structure) apply to the relationship of training incumbents and curates and to the development of true collaborative ministry among the whole people of God? (Leadership and Collaboration)
3. How am I accountable for my exercise of ministry? What formation and support structures do I need for my long-term effectiveness and health? A third question may be added here, How do I make best use of the support structures that are provided for me by the diocese or by those with whom I trained? (Personality and Character)
4. Where are you facing a difficult or tangled situation? How might the Quaker principles listed below help you find a way forward?

   - there is something of good, and thus of God, in everyone
   - people are the product of their social contexts

- for both ethical and effectiveness reasons, act in a friendly and cheerful manner towards those with whom you are in conflict
- try things out on the journey to a solution. Do not wait for the perfect answer. (Relationships)

5. What changes have taken place in your church recently? What do they say about the church's culture and core values, both its espoused values and its underlying assumptions? (Faith)
6. When did I last fall into 'Judger Self' thinking? How could I make more use of 'Learner Self' questions in future? (Personality and Character)

You may use questions more formally in a small group setting or in the supervision of others. Questions can be a way in which we empower others rather than instructing them. Where in our ministry, particularly in the areas of leadership and collaboration, could your exercise of your role and be more effective with greater use of questions?

Creating critical conversations

Related Learning Outcomes: Vocation, Faith and Quality of Mind

Look again at the grid on page 88 and use it to look over your last six supervision sessions. What sort of reflection have you engaged in with your incumbent? You could also do a similar exercise with team meetings if you are part of a ministry team. Now consider if you need to change the content of your supervision meetings to achieve a better range of reflective practice. If your incumbent insists that supervision should take place only immediately after events and not at a designated time, then this exercise could be especially pertinent.

Turn to the 'radio' on p. 90 and the questions designed to support the process of creating critical conversations try using this to help frame a discussion with your training incumbent, and/or for a supervision session looking at a recent experience in ministry that appears to lend itself to critical reflection.

Part 3 – Ministry

Time wisdom

Related Learning Outcomes: Spirituality, Personality and Character and Leadership

This chapter describes 'time wisdom'. As part of developing your own time wisdom try the exercises below.

Plot what you do and the extent to which it is lifegiving on a grid. Do the same with time and what is important for the kingdom in your context. Then reflect on the result.

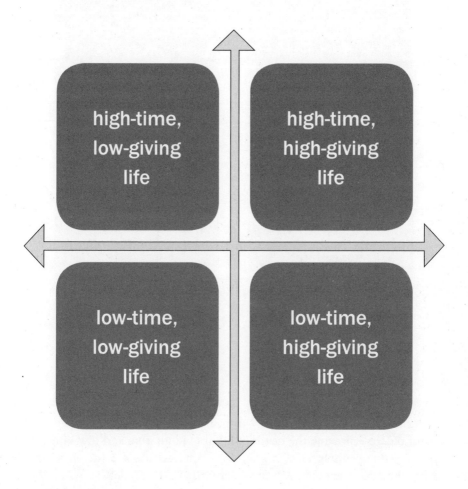

High-life giving and high time might be time spent with your family and/or engaged in exercise or, for some, pastoral visiting. High-time and low-life giving might mean writing up minutes or putting the parish magazine together etc. Are there enough activities to the right of the central line to sustain you? Do you feel guilty about these activities? Are there activities to the left of the central line that you could stop or give to someone for whom they would appear on the right side of the central line?

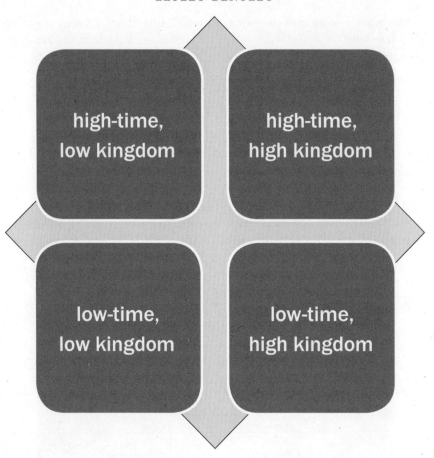

High time and high kingdom might mean writing your sermon or giving pastoral care following the death of a baby. High time and low kingdom might mean spending large amounts of time getting a poster just right rather than good enough. Are there activities in the top left quadrant that you could abandon? How do you feel about those in the top right? Are you giving them enough time or do rush yourself here?

Enabling ministry

Related Learning Outcomes: Personality and Character, Leadership, Mission and Evangelism

List the ways in which your ministry enables that of others. Consider with your supervisor how this element of your ministry could be further developed.

What vision have the PCC and church community articulated in your parish(es)? On the grid below plot where activities of the church support the vision, the activities where more could be done to further the vision, the new possibilities that are emerging that support the vision (or even encourage its development further) and where the vision is actually being hindered.

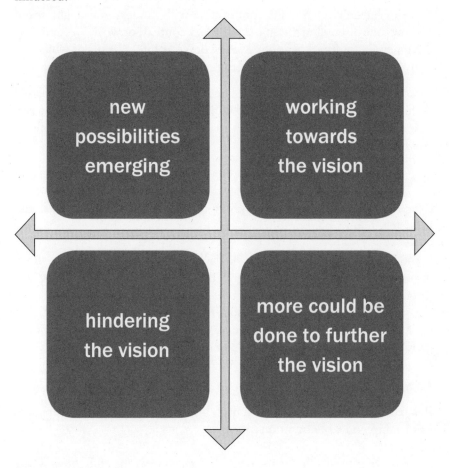

Discuss this with your supervisor.

Preaching

Related Learning Outcomes: Ministry in the C of E, Spirituality, Faith and Quality of Mind

The author has placed exercises and case studies within the chapter and the reader is referred back to these within their context.

Money

Related Learning Outcomes: Ministry in the C of E, Leadership and Collaboration, and Personality and Character

The author suggests:

> If you haven't yet become comfortable with money, you might spend some time discussing this in a supervisory context, or work through 'The Money Revolution' or 'Your Money or Your Life', details of which are given in the Further Reading section at the end.

Discover the ways in which issues of finance and stewardship are addressed within your current church(es) and reflect upon these. In a supervision session discuss this pattern with your incumbent, including any possibilities you have seen for improvement.

Law

Related Learning Outcomes: Ministry in the C of E, Relationships, and Leadership and Collaboration

Locate the Canons of the Church of England on the C of E website. Read through the chapters relating to Holy Orders and Baptism. Does anything here surprise you?

Locate the Church Representation Rules. Can you work out a time line for all that needs to be done before the day of your AGM (Annual meeting of parishioners and APCM)? What could be decided at each of these meetings?

Chairing meetings

Related Learning Outcomes: Ministry in the C of E, Relationships and Leadership and Collaboration

If you were responsible for the next PCC meeting at the church(es) where you serve what would you put on the agenda? What would others put on the agenda? To what would you give the greatest amount of time? Can you construct a timed agenda? What other preparation would you need to do if you were the chairperson? In what ways would you be exercising leadership if you were chairing this meeting? In what ways would you be furthering God's mission in your parish(es) through this agenda?

Share your thinking with your incumbent at a supervision session before the next PCC.

Index